CW01626911

JOHN WONNACOTT
A Biographical Study

First published in 2022 by Lund Humphries

Lund Humphries
The Alphabeta Building
18 Finsbury Square
London EC2A 1AH
UK

www.lundhumphries.com

John Wonnacott: A Biographical Study
© Charles Saumarez Smith, 2022
All rights reserved

978-1-84822-591-6

A Cataloguing-in-Publication record for this book is available from the British Library. All rights reserved. No part of this publication may be reproduced, stored in a retrieval system or transmitted in any form or by any means, electrical, mechanical or otherwise, without first seeking the permission of the copyright owners and publishers. Every effort has been made to seek permission to reproduce the images in this book. Any omissions are entirely unintentional, and details should be addressed to the publishers.

Charles Saumarez Smith has asserted his right under the Copyright, Designs and Patent Act, 1988, to be identified as the Author of this Work.

Front cover: *Self-Portrait with an Apple for G*, 2017, oil on canvas, 36.8 × 36.8cm (14 ½ × 14 ½ in), artist's collection.

Back cover: *Chalkwell Beach, Floodwater Overflow, Late Afternoon*, 1989–92, oil on board, 61 × 122 cm (24 × 48 in), British Council.

Copyedited by Robert Davies
Designed by Wolfe Hall
Set in Starling and Quadrant Mono
Printed in Estonia

Charles Saumarez Smith

JOHN WONNACOTT
A Biographical Study

LUND HUMPHRIES

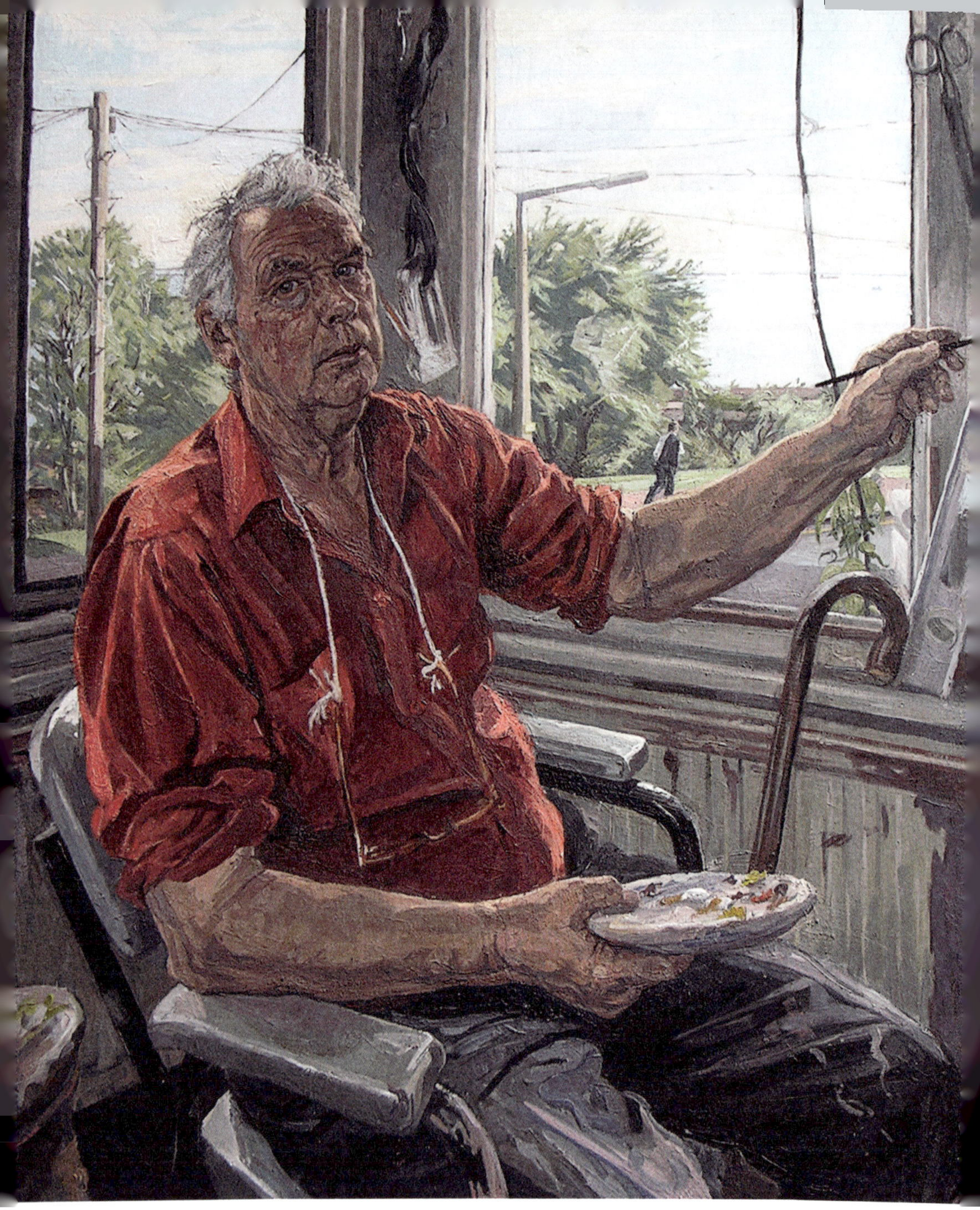

Self-Portrait, Summer Morning, The Red Shirt, 2003–5

Introduction

I first got to know John Wonnacott when I was Director of the National Portrait Gallery. Ever since, I have admired his devotion to the craft of painting, the science of exact observation, the mechanics of depiction, and his visual record of people, friends and the life of the Essex coast – what Lucian Freud (1922–2011) called his regional *comédie humaine*.

In the summer of 2019, John had an exhibition of his paintings in the Focal Point Gallery, the main exhibition space in Southend-on-Sea, his home town. I spent a very enjoyable day with him in early January 2019, including a picnic lunch of lamb and crab in his studio and an afternoon spent rootling around the two containers in which he stores his work, looking at the history of his life and previous work in preparation for a short essay which I had promised to write for the exhibition catalogue.[1]

As he delivered me back to his local railway station, Chalkwell, an old friend, Jonathan Mantle, with whom I had lost touch, was coming out. I introduced them. They have since become friends. Jonathan could not understand why John, a painter who is obviously so intensely serious as an artist, so committed to the idea of grand narrative in art and its construction in pigment, and such a brilliant visual technician, is not better known. That led directly to this book, which documents and records Wonnacott's life and work in order to reintroduce them to public attention.

I wrote this book in the early months of the Covid-19 lockdown as a record of his life and his total devotion to the practice of his art ever since his early days at the Slade: his encounter with Ernst Gombrich (1909–2001), who remained a devotee; his passionate study of the work of Old Master painters; his friendship with the artists of the School of London, including the teaching of Frank Auerbach (born 1931); and the poetry, combined with the science, of his study of the human figure in movement – in the studio, on a park bench and on the beach, always the subject of a strong formal composition, the idea of pictorial composition being the essential purpose of his art, more than mere likeness or documentary record.

Chapter 1

Early Life

John Wonnacott was born on 15 April 1940 in East Finchley, the son of an architect who spent the Second World War travelling the country designing and supervising the construction of radar and radio stations. His father belonged to the generation of architects who viewed architecture as a form of problem solving to make a better society. He was a very good draughtsman, doing beautiful architectural drawings in 4H pencil, but unlike John, he despised the work of modern artists, including Picasso (1881–1973), whom he thought 'a charlatan who would put the nose where the eyes should be'.[2]

John's parents came from Southend but they worked in London, where they met while his father was training for his architectural exams and his mother was working as a secretary in a law firm. They were both boarding at the same hotel in Islington. She was religious, low church, and inclined towards Quakerism, but oddly, given that she particularly disliked monks and nuns, she sent her son to Catholic schools on the grounds that they would provide a better education. He went first to the Mother Mary Auxiliary Convent on the East End Road (now a Jewish seminary), near where the family lived, and then to the Dominican monks at St Aloysius till he was ten. One of his earliest memories is 'of being told to draw a Catholic church with a golden sun above it and a Protestant church under an inverted black triangle', and he feels that the knowledge of Christian, and indeed Catholic, imagery has informed some of his later paintings, particularly after this period of his childhood came back to him in an opiate-induced delirium following surgery in 2011.[3]

Aged ten, Wonnacott was sent to a local East Finchley primary school, Holy Trinity, and from there he took the 11+ scholarship to University College School, the biggest and most prestigious in the neighbourhood, with strongly secular origins, located in grand buildings in Frognal in Hampstead and full of budding writers, mathematicians and scientists. He was encouraged to take an interest in art by one of the art masters, Mr Smaggersdale, who showed him pottery designed by Picasso and got him to draw figures in slip clay. But he was not only good at art. He was in the school rugby team until the age of 15, edited the school magazine, and did physics and chemistry at A level, showing an interest in science which has influenced his later fascination with optics.

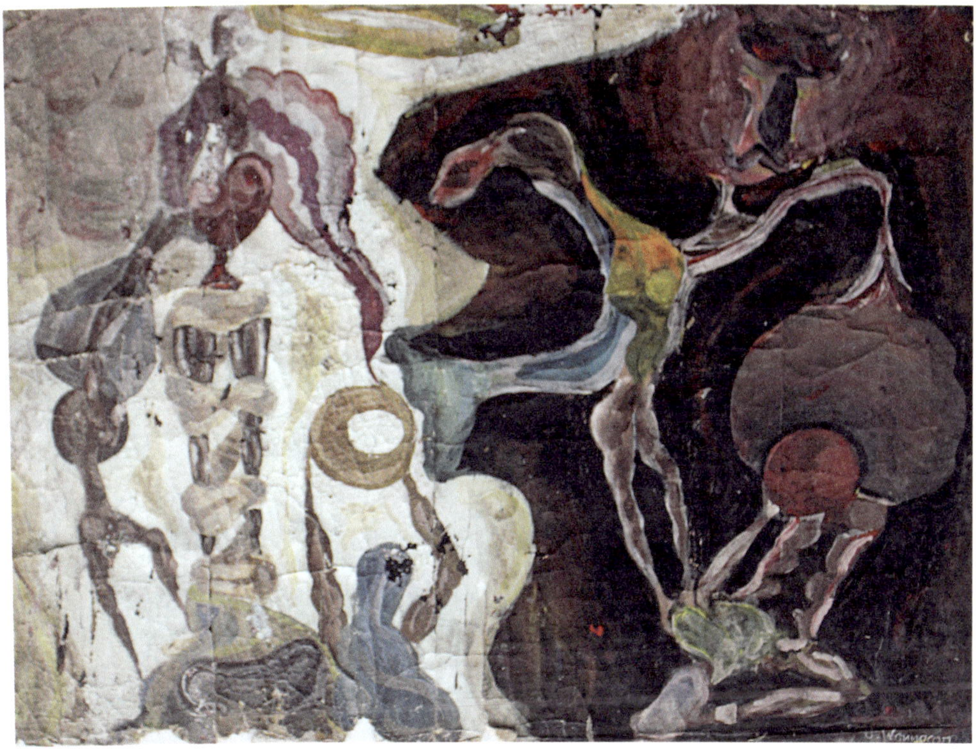

1. *Temptation*, 1953–4

It was another art master, Maurice Johnson, who persuaded Wonnacott that he should concentrate not on science, but on art. Johnson was one of those people who in the post-war period devoted themselves to teaching, a 'character' who had pretty much given up art in order to be able to concentrate on making guitars. Wonnacott describes him as the

> glamorous and outrageous Maurice Johnson, rarely seen without a fag and drink and immersed in the excitement of modern art. Maurice had been a minor (post-Picasso) romantic painter, friend of Ceri Richards (and of Michael Bentine) [and] kept a great art room library of gallery catalogues and Penguin monographs besides the usual Herbert Read, Gombrich and books of old masters ... In the evenings Maurice, short, dark and a James Mason lookalike, used to dress up in full Spanish costume and play around London clubs in a Spanish guitar and dance group, under the stage name of Maurici Juanes.[4]

It was Johnson who encouraged Wonnacott to paint:

> The breakthrough came when through all that turmoil of sex and religion of early adolescence I painted a picture called *Temptation*. Maurice immediately gave me all the board and oil paint I wanted. He also informed my parents that I should go to art school. They quite properly never forgave him, particularly as I was in the top science group.[5]

Temptation survives (fig.1), painted when he was only 13 or 14, in poster paint on sugar paper. It is not surprising that it made a great impression on Johnson – it is a free and swirling composition, which shows obvious ability and the fact that Wonnacott had already absorbed a surprising amount of imagery from Picasso and Edward Burra (1905–1976), an early influence on him and whose catalogues he used to study. There is a self-portrait drawing, done when Wonnacott was 16 (fig.2): he looks out at the world, coolly appraising it. This work already shows great confidence in his drawing skills. At 17, he drew *Gwen with Reginald*, Gwen being his mother and Reginald their cat, which had been acquired on a trip to Cornwall (fig.3).

2. *Self-Portrait*, 1956

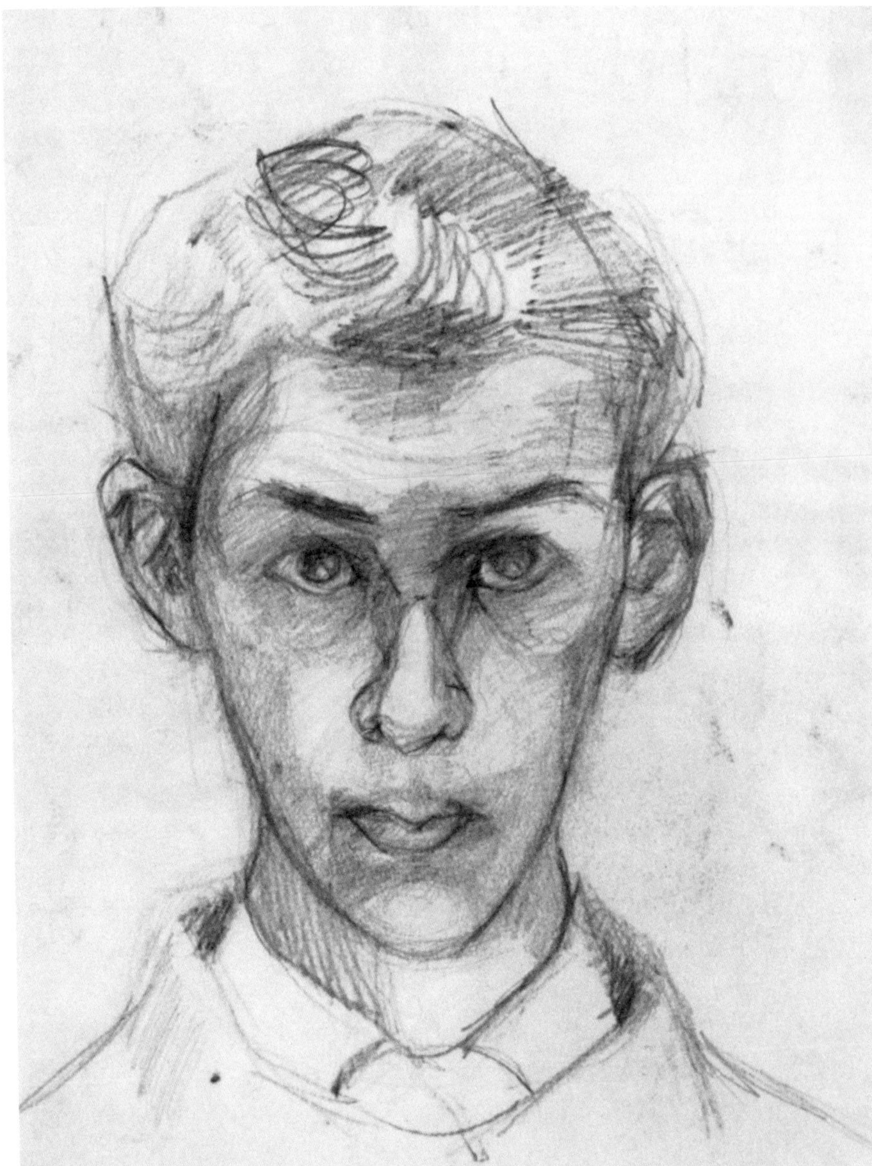

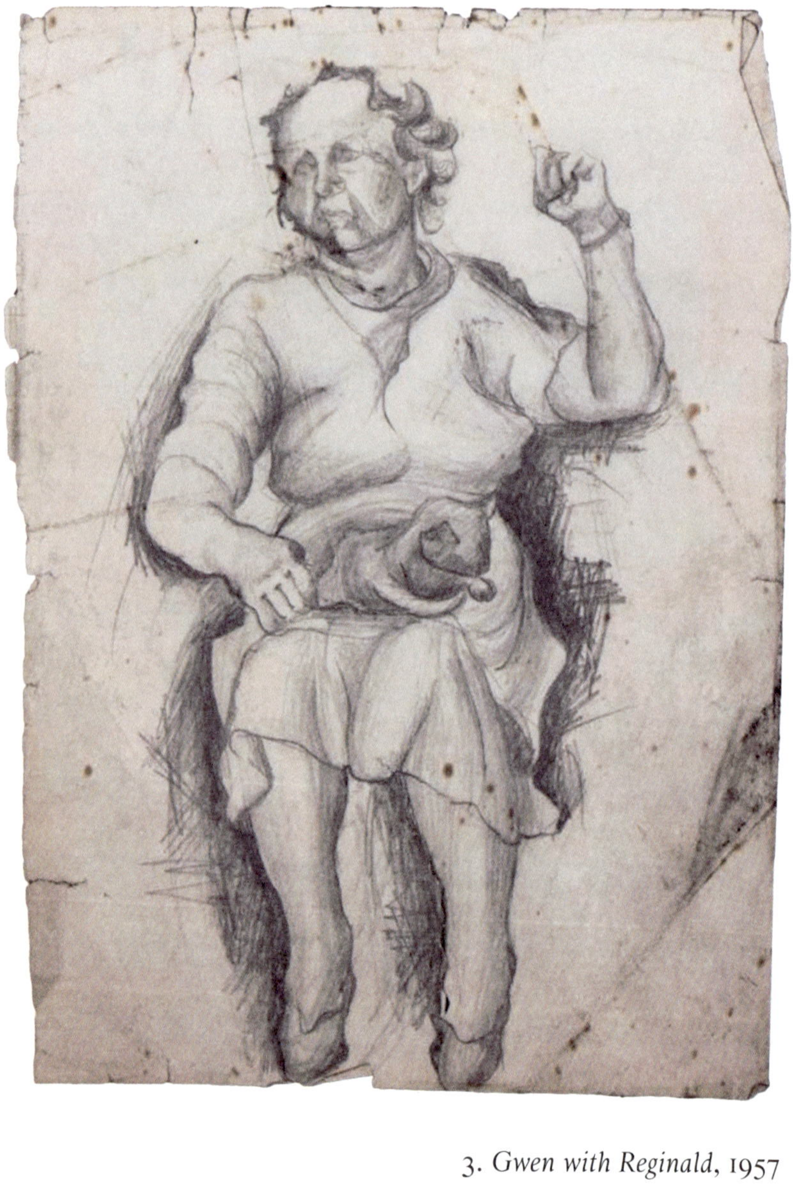

3. *Gwen with Reginald*, 1957

It was Johnson who introduced Wonnacott to the London art world by taking him and others to see work in the West End galleries, such that he had an unusually good knowledge and awareness of international artists by the time he was 16:

> One of the most important things that Maurice did was to take a group of us from the Art 6th form on a regular walk around the West End galleries looking at anything and everything – at Marlborough, Zwemmers, the Leicester etc. and of course the Beaux Arts in Bruton Place. That's where I saw my first Auerbachs, inches thick white on black nudes and tiny intense yellow profile heads on green. Maurice hated them but I couldn't get them out of my head. I also remember shows like [Constant] Permeke, [Evert] Lundquist and Craigie [Aitchison] and I particularly remember Helen [Lessore] hovering in black like a bird of prey on the first floor balcony looking down on us. I was in awe.[6]

The other influence on Wonnacott while he was at school was his friendship with Gilbert Jacobsen. He made friends with Gilbert on the rugby field. His mother Lulu was a painter who lived in a grand house in Blenheim Road in St John's Wood, a smarter part of town than where Wonnacott's own parents were in East Finchley (he says that 'Lulu was a great bohemian snob and regarded my family as hopelessly suburban'). He describes the experience of visiting their house aged 12:

> My house in Finchley didn't have pictures. My father did I think have a Russell Flint print – most architects at that time were fascinated by watercolour. At Lulu's, pictures hung wall to wall, Claude Rogers, Freddie Gore (a friend of Lulu's), Camden Town and best of all terrific Danish paintings from her husband's family. Lulu was herself a serious painter and had been in Paris in the great days with Picasso and others – she didn't like him.[7]

In spite of his aptitude for science, Wonnacott applied in his A level year to the Slade School of Art, part of University College

London, the parent body of his school. He was turned down – maybe, he thinks, because both he and his paintings were felt to be too unsophisticated, displaying a sense of innocent enthusiasm about the practice of art, a certain type of eagerness which was a contrast to some of the world-weariness and cultivated ennui of the Slade, as he later found, as well as elements of the social snobbery which he had first experienced in St John's Wood. Luckily, through Lulu Jacobsen, he had met Claude Rogers (1907–1979), who taught at the Slade and was involved with its admissions. Rogers encouraged William Coldstream (1908–1987), the head of the Slade, to take a second look at Wonnacott's work and he was offered a place.

Chapter 2

The School of London

The Slade School of Fine Art has been much the biggest influence on Wonnacott and the way he thinks about and practises art. He arrived in October 1958, and, since he was encouraged to stay on for an extra year, did not leave until June 1963.

It is worth exploring the Slade's ethos and the nature of its system of teaching in order to understand the world that Wonnacott still inhabits: its commitment to an intense analysis and description of the human form and, to a lesser extent, the physical world through analytical drawing; and its belief that looking, thinking about the nature of looking, and describing what one is looking at lies at the heart of the practice of art and is what makes it worthwhile.

During Wonnacott's time, the Slade Professor of Fine Art was William Coldstream, a cool and methodical painter, but somewhat neurotic and highly strung as a person, who helped to establish what is still regarded as 'the Slade method'. Coldstream had learned that method when he was himself a student at the Slade in the late 1920s, taught by Henry Tonks, who had been trained as a surgeon. Tonks had an utter disdain for most aspects of contemporary art and a disciplined view of observation, telling Tristram Hillier (1905–1983) when he was a student: 'If you wish to occupy yourself in making geometrical patterns, you have no need of my models, and I will tell the secretary to give you a room of your own in which you can draw cubes, circles, squares, triangles, or whatever else you may fancy, but where you will be unable to corrupt your fellow-students with this obscene nonsense.'[8]

After a period working for the GPO Film Unit making documentary films, Coldstream returned to the practice of painting and, with financial help from the art historian Kenneth Clark (1903–1983), who was a neighbour in Hampstead, he was able to develop his ideas through his teaching at the so-called Euston Road School. This was a school of painting and drawing which Coldstream, Claude Rogers and Victor Pasmore (1908–1998) established first at 12 Fitzroy Square and, from February 1938, in 'a huge beautiful disused car showroom' near Warren Street Underground station at 314–16 Euston Road.[9]

The teaching at Euston Road consisted of an analytical style of observation, sometimes involving measurement, in which the human figure was treated with clinical and observational detachment, as if the practice of painting was a science as much as an art. It lent itself to documentary realism and to portraiture, based on the fact that, in the arguments between realism and abstraction in the 1930s, Coldstream belonged to the group who, as his friend W.H. Auden wrote, 'scrapped Significant Form, and voted for Subject'.[10]

The ideas and beliefs of the Euston Road School developed and, to an extent, indoctrinated into young artists through the discipline of drawing, have been a dominant trend in painting ever since: the School had an interest in the depiction of human form in a way that can be dry, but is based on the belief that providing a visual record of the human figure is fundamentally important and what art has been, and should be, about.

Coldstream was a distant figure, an effective academic administrator and good committee man – a trustee of the National Gallery and the Tate, and author of what was known as 'the First Coldstream Report', published in October 1960, which treated art as a subject of academic study, required qualifications at A level to enter art school, and established a three-year Diploma in Art and Design, which became the standard qualification for art schools.[11] This was regarded by some, including Wonnacott, as the death of the art school, which had been ruled by people with strong visual but not necessarily intellectual skills, but was now subject to the more formal disciplines of the academic world. As it happens, Wonnacott was, and remains, in some ways, a traditional painter, rooted in the formal traditions of the Slade, who has reacted against the orthodoxies of modernism and has a strong interest in the formal composition of pictures and the science of perception. He talks of an 'intellectual, aesthetic and physical discipline of drawing', which requires close observational analysis. He believes that skill in painting and drawing is learned by the brain through the training of the eye – an aspect of creative vision treating spatial design and perspective geometry as part of a single aesthetic discipline.[12]

Coldstream did not involve himself much in teaching at the Slade. But he was nevertheless a strong presence when it came to establishing the intellectual ethos of the school, as Wonnacott remembers:

> A vivid memory ... is of the unscheduled appearances by Professor Sir William Coldstream hovering above

us on the balcony leading from his ground-floor office. I don't think Bill ever talked to us first years individually but we lived in awe of the perceptive dry wit and caustic analysis delivered through maestro performances in his open school crits that were great occasions in the Slade calendar.[13]

Wonnacott has good memories of the discipline involved in being at the Slade, beginning with time spent in the life room:

In the first year we drew in the large basement life room along with students from all other years who also wanted to draw. This included people like Terry Setch and friends who spent most of their time working on vast American canvases on the upstairs corridor. The life room was manned by a number of distinguished draughtsmen teachers, most of whose names escape me, though I do remember Tom Monnington and I think I still have a foot drawing by Nuttal Smith on one of my figures. The poses changed daily and I still have a number of drawings from that time.[14]

Alongside the life room, there were two days of drawing classes each week, conducted by Patrick George (1923–2016), who had been a student at Edinburgh College of Art before joining the Royal Naval Reserve and studying after the war at Camberwell, where he had been taught by Coldstream, Pasmore and Rogers. Coldstream had invited him to join him at the Slade, where he taught first-year students for many years. Wonnacott does not think that Patrick George particularly liked him or ever came to value his work:

For two days a week we also worked on a first-year drawing course run by Patrick George. I remember that it started with making a line to stand for a piece of string lying on a flat surface. This didn't much interest me though it did encourage a solid unprissy carpenter's line ... Patrick taught us objective measurement with a pencil held at arm's length against a virtual picture plane and we were encouraged to draw sight size. In the downstairs life room I always drew much larger, allowing the figure to fill an A3 sheet of paper. I drew there with charcoal. We drew mostly from still life arrangements with Patrick as I remember it, shapes between bottles etc. We were also encouraged to draw casts in the antique room, which was great. I think this sort of drawing activity was happening at small and large art schools all over the country at this time, based on the Slade course. I realised when involved in this discipline that the virtual picture plane was the equivalent of Van Gogh's perspective frame illustrated in his letters, so I threw myself in without reserve.[15]

Second-year teaching was conducted by Andrew Forge (1923–2002), an exact contemporary of Patrick George at the Downs School near Malvern. Forge, too, had been a student at Camberwell after the war, before Coldstream appointed him to the Slade in 1950. He was a more intellectual figure, writing about art for the *New Statesman* and *Studio International* and, in 1958, he curated an exhibition of the work of David Bomberg (1890–1957) for the Arts Council. Again, Wonnacott has good and clear memories of the nature of Forge's teaching and his encouragement later in his career:

In our second year we still spent most of our time in the basement life room but worked for two sessions of about three weeks each with Andrew Forge, painting the nude from a fixed position – our first painting at the Slade and the longest I had ever taken on a single pose. I still value both paintings and Andrew in particular began to take me seriously from this time. In both of these 30 inches by 20 inches paintings the nude filled the board with organic paint and I remember being very influenced by my admiration for early Kokoschka – he later visited the school and my admiration for him vanished.[16]

In his second year at the Slade, John painted *The White Nude, Marjorie* (fig.4), a work of considerable authority, with roughly handled, scumbled paint, much influenced by what Wonnacott describes as 'my then hero worship of Oskar Kokoschka'.[17]

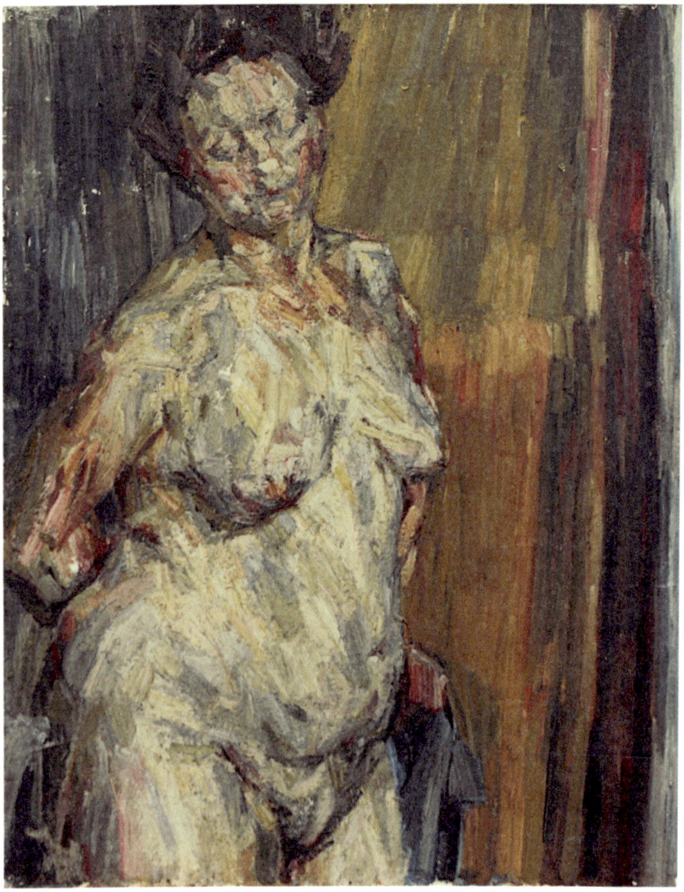

4. *The White Nude, Marjorie*, 1959

But much the biggest influence on John and his work during his time at the Slade was Frank Auerbach, who taught a six-week course on drawing before being employed formally as a part-time, one-day-a-week tutor – he thinks – in October 1963.[18] Auerbach himself remembers how one model for the informal classes arrived 'in formal "office" dress, lay down on the mattress, posed well while the students worked, and kept her distance from everyone during breaks. At the end the students bought her a box of chocolates to show their appreciation and she burst into tears.'[19]

At the time, Auerbach was in his early thirties, but already well established as a painter, for example exhibiting at the Beaux Arts Gallery in the summer of 1962 alongside his close friend and ally Leon Kossoff (1926–2019) and the Swedish painter Evert Lundquist

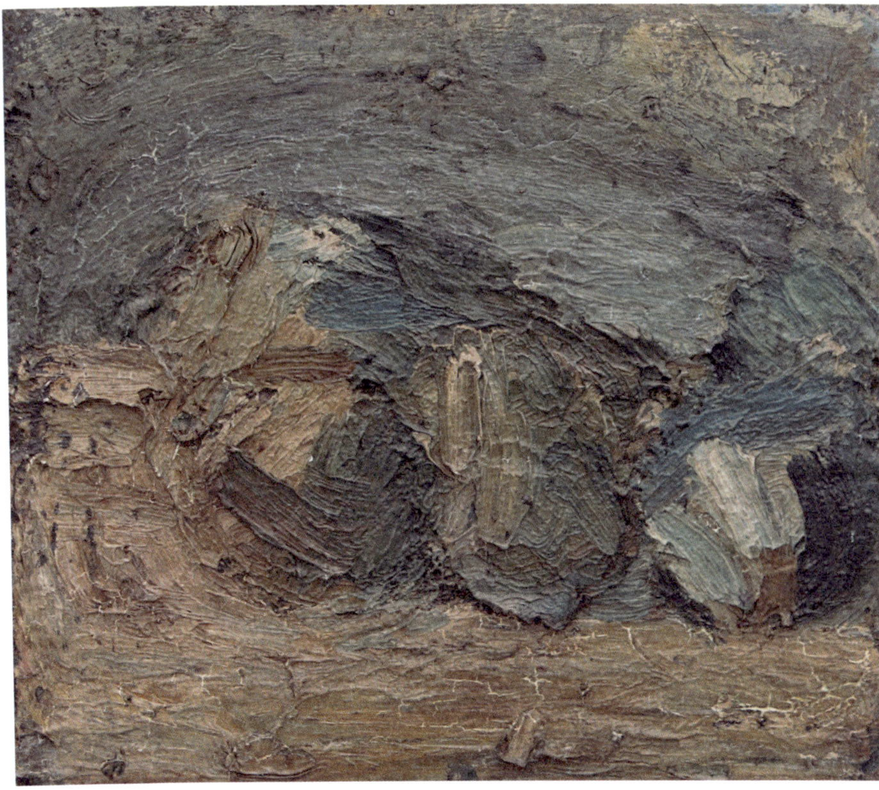

5. *Cooking Apples*, 1962

(1904–1994). He had studied painting under Bomberg at Borough Polytechnic, and went to St Martin's School of Art in 1948 and the Royal College of Art in 1952. His first exhibition at the Beaux Arts Gallery was in January 1956 and he was regarded by many, including Wonnacott, as the most exciting and adventurous young painter of the time. Auerbach was scruffy, still with a guttural German accent, with a studio in Mornington Crescent, passionate not only about the practice of art, but also knowledgeable about its history. As Wonnacott describes it:

> In our third year, those of us who were still determined to work from the model could choose to paint in one of a series of small life rooms under the supervision of one of the finest life painters in the country. I queued from the crack of dawn to secure my place in Frank Auerbach's room where he would turn up twice a week armed with catalogues

of Soutine, Rembrandt, Matisse or whoever he was currently absorbed in. Frank made the act of painting the most important of human endeavours and expanded the possibilities of both looking and inventing.[20]

Wonnacott has described Auerbach's influence as being 'to encourage us to see the figure as part of the life room landscape of easels, heaters and other students etc., to be organised across the floor and wall space – rather than allowing the figure to swell up and take over the canvas picture space'.[21] Auerbach's influence is obvious in one of Wonnacott's paintings which survives from this period, *Cooking Apples* (fig.5). With thickly applied and scumbled paint, the picture is as much about surface as form.

The other big influence on Wonnacott was in his fourth year at the Slade when he was taught by Michael Andrews (1928–1995), who had been a star student at the Slade in the early 1950s, taught by Coldstream, and still did part-time teaching there while developing his own career as a painter. At the time, Andrews was deeply interested in the idea of the group portrait, including *The Family in the Garden* (fig.6), a detailed depiction of his family at home in Glebe Road, Norwich, where his father, an insurance clerk, worked for the Norwich Union. It is a visual and anthropological study of family life, the artist's relationship to his family and their relationship to one another, a meticulous documentary record.

Alongside the formal teaching of drawing, there were compulsory art history lectures on Friday afternoons. Ernst Gombrich was Durning-Lawrence Professor at University College London from 1956 to 1959, when he went to Harvard, and was working on *Art and Illusion*, based on the Andrew Mellon lectures which he had given in Washington in 1956 and published in 1960. Gombrich reinforced the sense of the seriousness of the practice of art and its roots in the psychology of perception, contributing to an interest in the science of optics which Wonnacott has maintained over several decades. Both Wonnacott and his close friend John Lessore (born 1939) were, and still are, passionate about the study of art history, taking themselves off while they were students and ever since to the National Gallery and the British Museum to study works of art in depth and to draw them, which was regarded as a central part of their training. As Lessore writes:

```
My influences were van Gogh, Gaudier[-Brzeska],
Sickert, whose work John never related to. I think
he was more Flemish and Florentine orientated and
I more Venetian and French. It may be this has
remained, except we are mad about all great
western art and frequently visit things together,
usually liking the same things.[22]
```

I describe the circumstances of the formation of Wonnacott's artistic style and his evolution as an artist because it demonstrates the extent to which he belonged, and still belongs, to the milieu which R.B. Kitaj (1932–2007) described in 1976 as 'the School of London', a description which those who belong to the School resist, as they don't like the idea that they belong to any group.[23] But the group does have certain obvious characteristics.

The first is ties of friendship. They are aware of, and sometimes criticise, each other's work. John Wonnacott and John Lessore belong to a younger generation than those artists who are the best-known members of the group – Bacon, Freud, Auerbach, Kossoff and Andrews – but they got to know them when they were young, since they were all in one way or another associated with the Beaux Arts Gallery, which had been run since 1951 by John Lessore's mother, Helen Lessore (1907–1994). Although she is said not to have been very businesslike in the way she managed the

6. Michael Andrews, *The Family in the Garden*, 1960–62

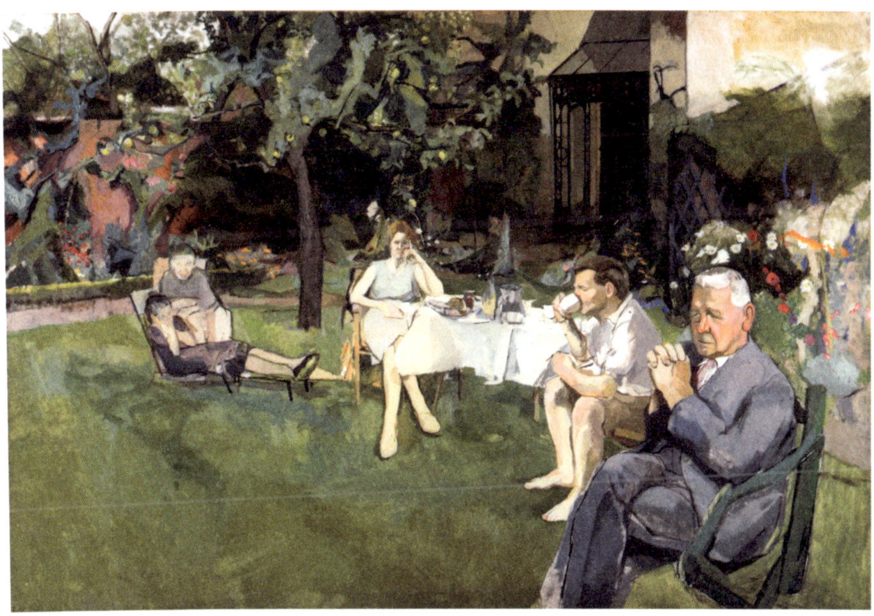

finances of the gallery, she was fiercely loyal to those artists she chose to represent, beginning with Francis Bacon (1909–1992) – whose work she first showed in 1953, after which he moved to the Hanover Gallery – followed by Frank Auerbach and Michael Andrews, first shown in 1956, and Leon Kossoff in 1957. They used her upstairs gallery in Bruton Place (she lived downstairs) as somewhere in which to rendezvous before going off drinking together in Soho and, through his friendship with John Lessore and exhibitions of their work, not to mention Auerbach's inspirational teaching, Wonnacott was deeply influenced by this group in his thinking about art.

The second characteristic of members of the group is their view of themselves as outsiders. They do not particularly want, or expect, to be part of the more fashionable art world. Their duty lies in their studio, where they devote themselves to the craft and practice of their art, day after day, week after week. The satisfaction of their lives is the everyday activity of looking, painting, looking again, not exactly recording and documenting the world as they see it, but reconfiguring and interpreting it through the medium of oil paint. Frank Auerbach said of the work of Michael Andrews that 'Mike does these things that at first look like old railway travel posters, but when you really look at them they're truly beautiful pictures.'[24] The same could be said of Wonnacott.

The third characteristic of the group is that its members feel they belong to a long tradition and are not part of a more ephemeral avant-garde. In 1986, Helen Lessore wrote *Partial Testament: Essays on Some Moderns in the Great Tradition*, which included essays on Andrews, Auerbach, Bacon, Freud and Kossoff. If the world of art is to be divided between the avant-garde and those who look to a long tradition, then it is the latter whose work will survive.

This was the milieu in which Wonnacott's attitude to art was formed. These are the ideas and beliefs to which he has devoted his art.

Chapter 3

The Family

In terms of a career move in the art world, Wonnacott could scarcely have made a worse choice than going to live in Essex while he was at the Slade, persuading his parents that he could live at home in Leigh-on-Sea and use their garage as a studio. So much of the art world revolves round London, the galleries in Bond Street, the pubs and bars of Soho, and, in the last three decades, the move into East London, that Wonnacott's determination to live in Leigh-on-Sea has made him stand apart, despite a growing interest in the vocabulary and aesthetics of coastal Essex.[25]

Wonnacott's parents came from Southend-on-Sea, a large seaside town on the north side of the Thames estuary, east of London, the nearest place that Londoners could breathe sea air, with late Georgian terraces high up on the riverfront, overlooking 1920s hotels, with streets of Victorian housing behind and a long pier stretching out into the Thames.

Wonnacott's grandparents had lived there. His paternal grandfather had been reasonably well off, but died young of lung damage. His grandmother had then remarried, so there was a half-aunt born in Southend, who became a cutter in the fashion trade and made things for her local amateur dramatic society in Muswell Hill ('Joyce could knock off a pretend Rembrandt or a lobster or gilt chair in hours').[26] Joyce babysat John and his siblings once a week. His maternal grandfather was trained as a carpenter, but was gassed in the First World War, and thereafter could only earn a living 'working casually on a Leigh cockle boat and as a pleasure boat skipper taking holiday makers on Estuary round trips from Chalkwell Beach'.[27] His grandmother ran a boarding house in Chalkwell, a suburb between Southend and the old fishing village of Leigh-on-Sea, and was a member of various non-conformist groups, 'including Baptist, Wesleyan and sects like the Seventh Day Adventists'.[28]

As a child, Wonnacott was close to his grandparents. His family used to drive down to Chalkwell from Finchley to visit every other weekend in their Ford Eight. In his last year at the Slade, he began to work on a painting which ended up taking the next 11 years – a big picture of his family in Southend, which he used as a way of documenting and coming to terms with his suburban background (he had been patronised by the more worldly students at the Slade such as Patrick Procktor, 1936–2003). It was partly an exercise in tracking them through time, but more a way of teaching himself to paint through a long process of intensive, analytical, self-reflective observation, not only looking at each member of the family in turn, but simultaneously an exercise in creating a relationship between observation and pictorial record: an interest not in pure painting, but in painting as a science. It is a wide-angle record of his life, the scale enlarged while he was painting it (fig.7).

The picture was, as Wonnacott is the first to acknowledge, much influenced by Michael Andrews's *The Family in the Garden* as a depiction of the sociology and dynamics of family life, based on a belief, strong at the time, that the arts should be about the record of reality without sentimentalisation, evident also in the writings of Iris Murdoch and Muriel Spark. The artist describes what led him into this hugely ambitious venture:

> Somewhere around the end of my fourth year, Helen Lessore, whose Beaux Arts Gallery had become my second art school, put on a show of Mike Andrews's paintings that included *The Family in the Garden*. This kick-started my own painting *The Family* that occupied me through the sixties ... Just as I had been bowled over by Helen's show of Frank Auerbach during the time he was teaching us, I knew that I must now learn from Mike how to slow down and rethink the whole painting process. The looking and the inventing were no less instinctive, but now a part of me was forever on my shoulder, watching and analysing the relationship between the two processes, occasionally advised by a reticent and nervous Mike Andrews offering, for example, his thoughts on the purpose of a particular brushstroke.[29]

This gives a sense of how Wonnacott was in retreat from Auerbach's view of the world, expressed through the brushstroke, deep pigment added in layers, towards Michael Andrews's cooler appraisal of the world, trying to create a more neutral science of depiction, using painting as an examination of the neurology of vision.

A number of drawings and preliminary studies survive for *The Family*. They show Wonnacott, first of all, thinking about the architecture of the setting, as in *Crescent Road 1* (fig.8); and there is a self-portrait of him painting the garden (fig.9).

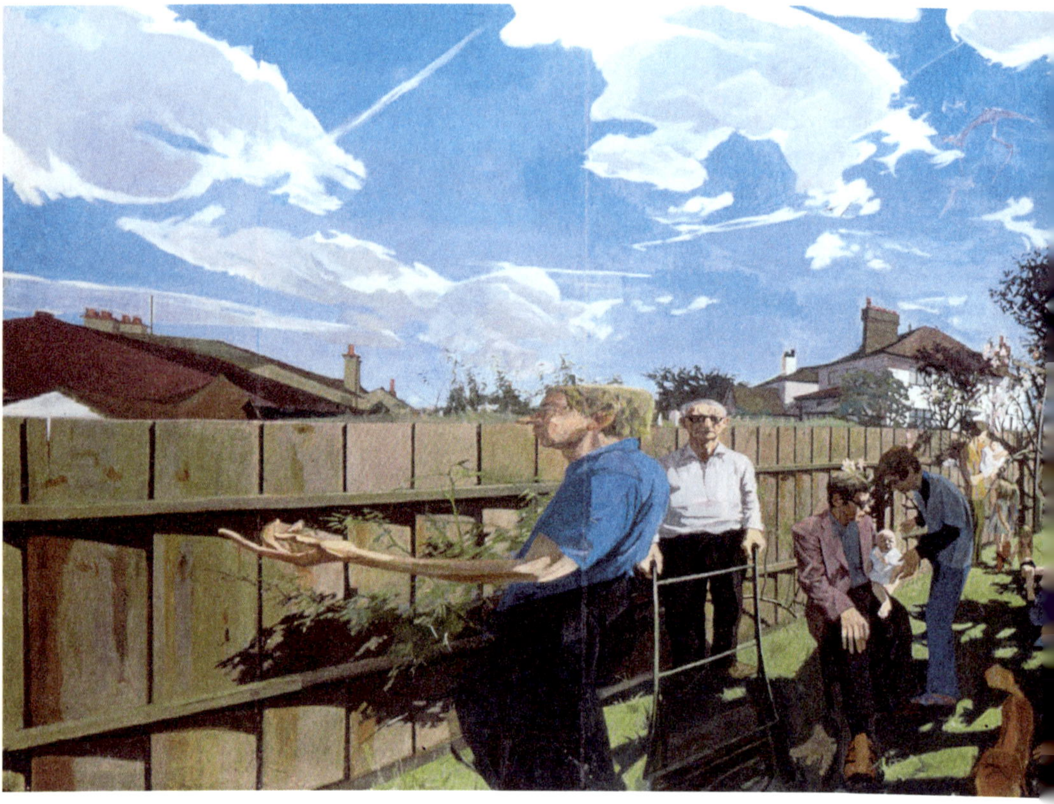

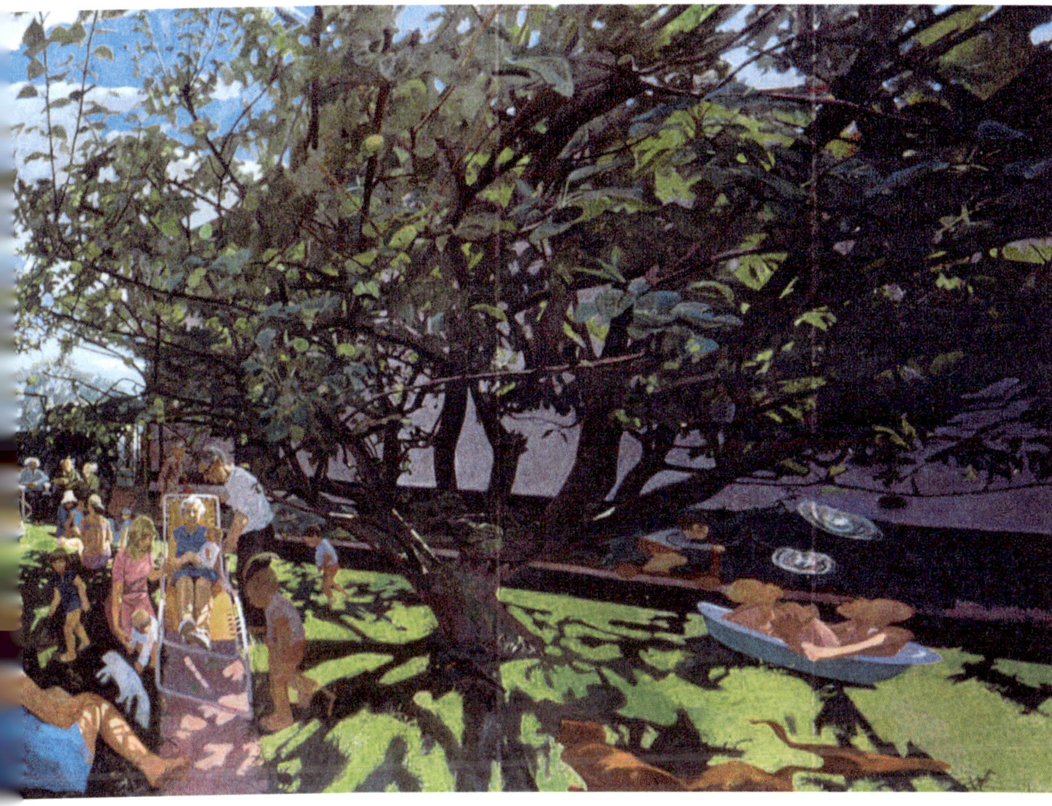

7. *The Family*, 1963–74

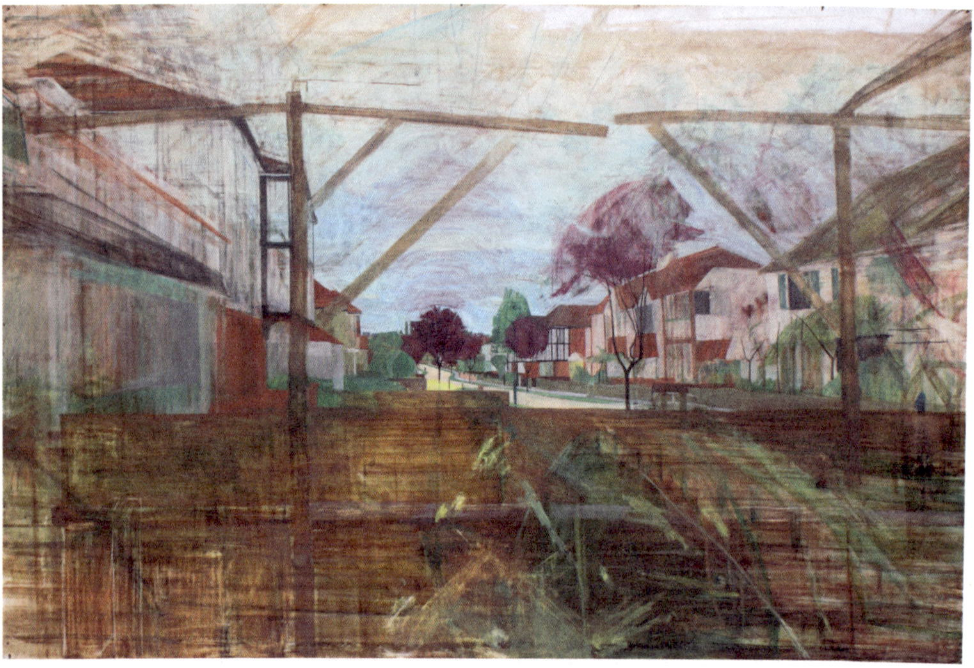

8. *Crescent Road I*, 1964–6

9. *Crescent Road*, 1963–76

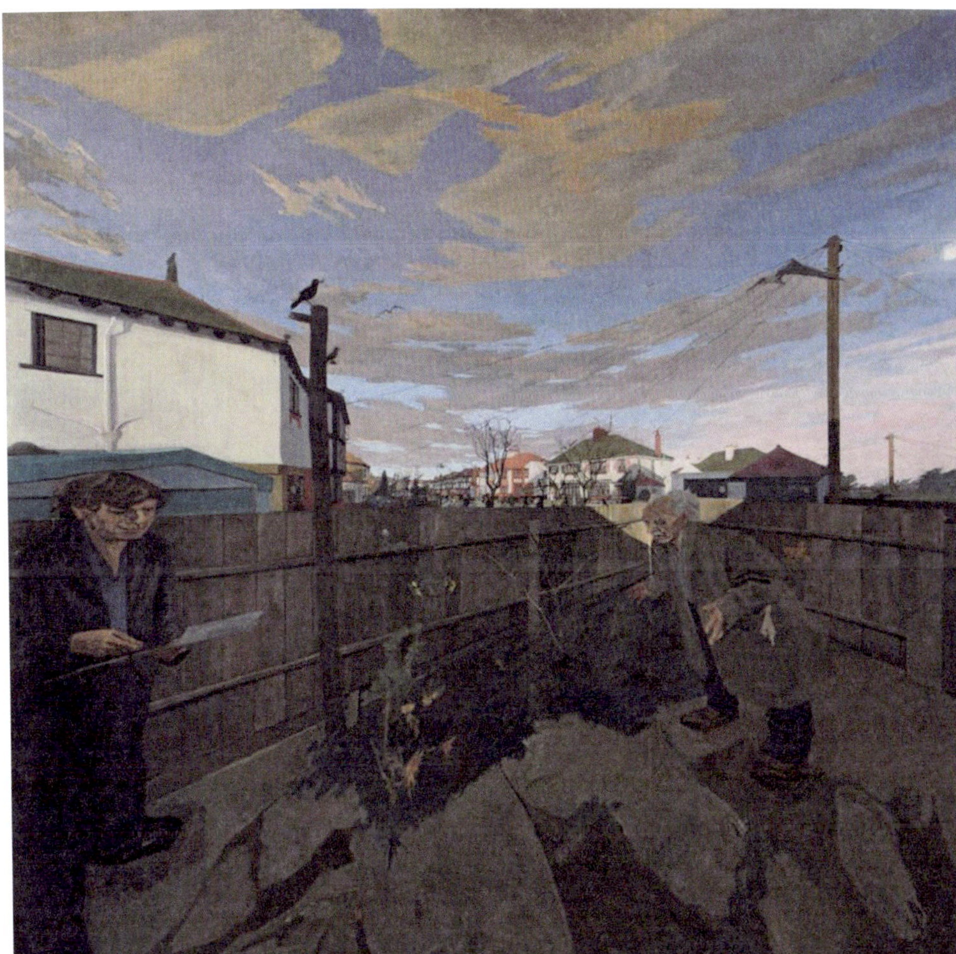

10. Three studies for *The Family, Whole Painting 2*, 1970

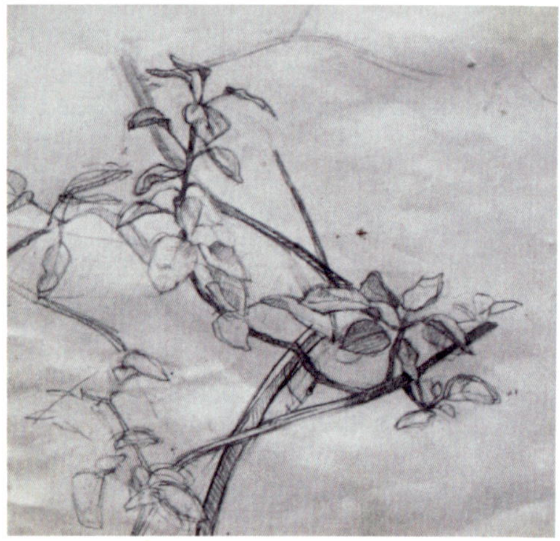

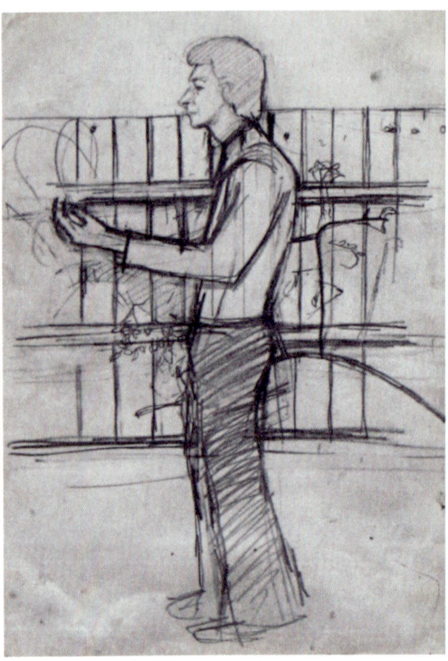

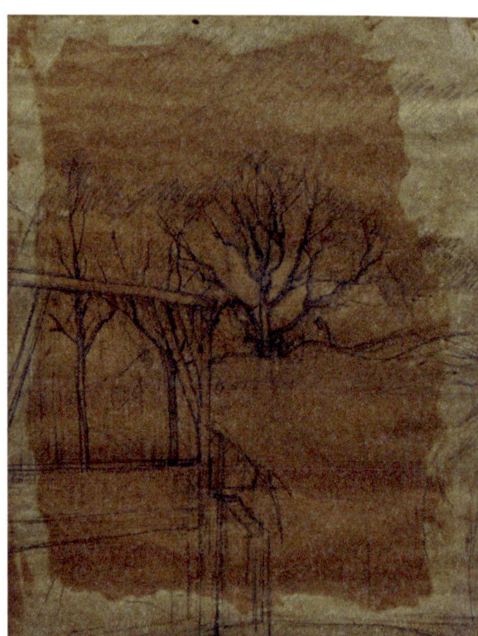

By 1970, he had a sense as to what the larger composition might be, incorporating the different generations of his family and details from the garden in a wide-angle view (fig.10). Wonnacott regards this picture, for good reason, as his first *chef d'oeuvre*:

> *The Family* became my 'masterpiece' in the medieval sense of the word. It enabled me to sort out the areas of painting that would occupy me for the rest of my working life and prove to myself that I could become worthy of inclusion in the great tradition of Western panting. I came to value the difference between painting and other great disciplines – of music and literature. Painting can't deal directly with the passage of linear time, [whereas] the writer can lead you through a narrative from beginning to end or allow a musical theme to develop and change over the hours of the performance. The painter must compress those millions of visual moments as skies move, trees change colour, children grow up and parents grow old, into a single newly invented moment of time. An invention that must hit the spectator as hard as any [Jackson] Pollock or [Barnett] Newman before you are drawn in to read the image moment by moment across the surface. The camera becomes a vital tool for reinforcing memory of those moments that drew my attention over the eleven years of the picture's making. You are looking at the passage of time when you view the painting.[30]

Wonnacott worked and worked at this picture. While his contemporaries were enjoying swinging London, he was in a back garden in Chalkwell, trying to work out his own way of seeing and documenting the world, much more complex in the way that it operated than any photograph.

In 1974, Wonnacott exhibited two works closely related to *The Family*, in a big survey exhibition of British painting, *British Painting '74*, held at the Hayward Gallery. Andrew Forge, who had remained a supporter of his work, asked 24 painters to select ten painters each. The painters had to be either at least five years younger or five years older, to ensure that they were not just friends. Forge wanted the exhibition to be, as he described it, 'heterogeneous and contradictory' and 'to cut a deep slice through the ant-hill of painting in this country', documenting the full range of art practice of the time, not privileging one aspect of it, displaying a generosity of spirit as to how the contemporary art world might be shown, led by artists themselves.[31]

The first of Wonnacott's paintings shown in 1974 was titled *Trees and Grandfather* (1973), which he now calls *Watching the Grandfather*, and dates from 1970 (it may be earlier still, because he thinks it was painted in 'about the third year into my working on *The Family*'[32]), a study as much of tree and foliage as it is of the artist in the bottom right-hand corner studying his sleeping grandfather (fig.11). *Elms on Marine Parade* (1974) was the other, now titled *Winter on Marine Parade* and dated 1972–4 (fig.12). It shows his father, who was dying, standing in the garden outside their house, hands behind his back, winter trees lining the street. Wonnacott's pictures were hung in Gallery 4 with work by Keith Vaughan (1912–1977), Leon Kossoff, Peter Blake (born 1932), Allen Jones (born 1937) and Anthony Green (born 1939). Wonnacott only remembers its proximity to work by Maggi Hambling (born 1945), who had been a student at the Slade in the late 1960s, and Frank Bowling (born 1934), a student at the Royal College of Art when Wonnacott was at the Slade. The effect of Wonnacott's picture and its quality was remembered ten years later in a review by Giles Auty (1934–2020), the painter-cum-critic who wrote for the *Spectator* (he knew Wonnacott from the fact that they both taught at Epsom College of Art):

> When I first saw John Wonnacott's paintings in *British Painting '74* at the Hayward, the bubble exhaled by the dying lungs of Late Modernism had yet to burst. Given the oddly oppressive climate of that time, his paintings showed remarkable qualities of independence and integrity.[33]

In 1975, *The Family* was selected for the Royal Academy's Summer Exhibition, with a committee chaired by its then President, Thomas Monnington (1902–1975), and including John Aldridge (1905–1983), Edward Bawden (1903–1989), Norman Blamey (1914–2000) and Anthony Green, a young painter only a year older than Wonnacott and at the Slade just before him.[34] At the time, the Summer Exhibition was still regarded as a good venue in which a young painter could show his or her work, independently

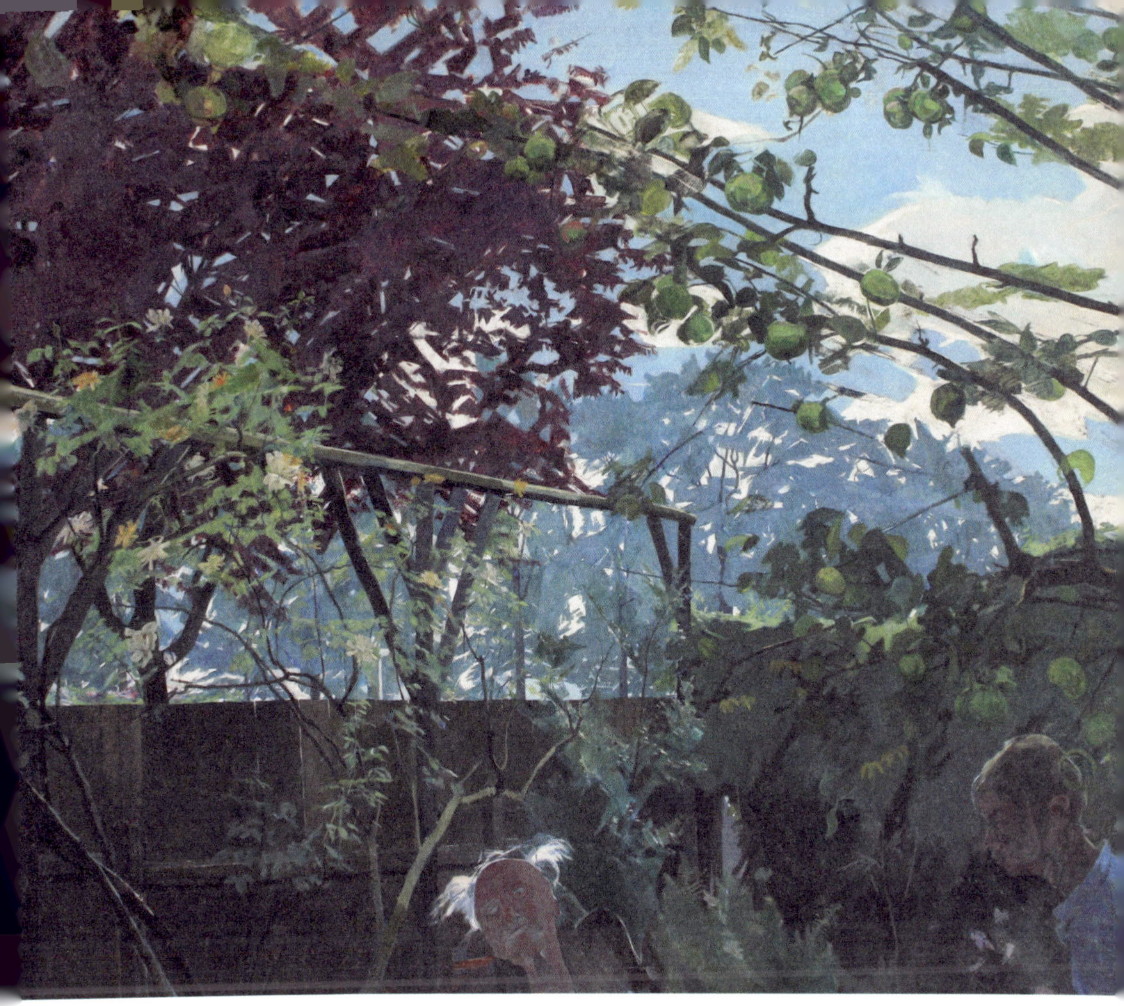

11. *Watching the Grandfather*, sketch for *The Family*, *c.*1970

of the Cork Street galleries, in spite of its conservatism. *The Family* was shown on the end wall of Gallery 3, the largest gallery and the first that members of the public normally see, a place of great honour, where it was hung above a big picture by John Bratby (1928–1992).

The painter John Hoyland (1934–2011), a student in the Royal Academy Schools in the late 1950s, admired the painting and included it two years later in a survey exhibition, *British Painting 1952–77*, held at the Royal Academy in autumn 1977 to celebrate the Queen's Silver Jubilee. The picture made a big impression. The critic Lynda Morris, a friend and supporter of Wonnacott since getting to know him at Norwich School of Art in the 1980s, remembers seeing the work for the first time:

> It was by far the largest painting in the exhibition and strangely distorted at the edges. To see it properly you had to find the central position in front of the painting in an always crowded room. To understand it, you had to stand quite close to the middle of the painting to allow the distortions

12. *Winter on Marine Parade*, 1972–4

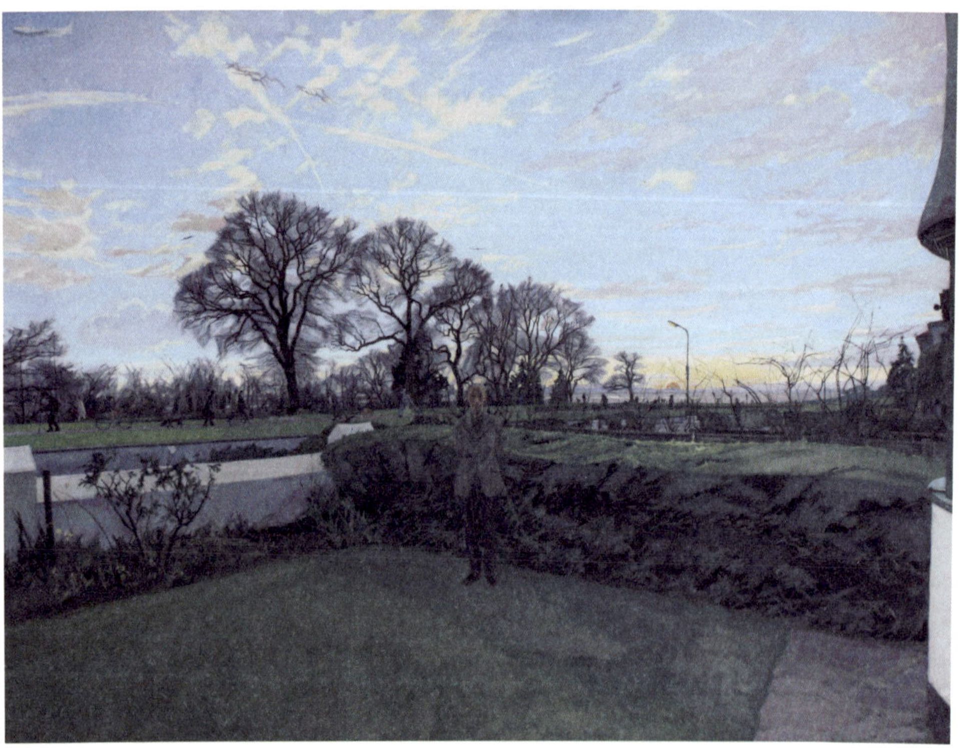

towards the edges to be normalised, at the edge of your own field of vision. It was figurative but not painterly.[35]

It was as a result of this painting that the London art world became aware of a new talent, just at the moment when artists were once again interested in the issues surrounding drawing and figuration, and were moving away from minimalism and conceptualism, as had been evident in an exhibition of works on paper, mainly those selected by R.B. Kitaj for the Arts Council Collection, but supplemented by loans, held the previous year at the Hayward Gallery. It was in the catalogue of this exhibition, *The Human Clay*, that the term 'the School of London' first gained currency. Kitaj made the case that you 'shouldn't listen to the fools who say either that pictures of people can be of no consequence or that painting is finished':

> There are artistic personalities in this small island more unique and strong and I think more numerous than anywhere in the world outside America's jolting artistic vigor. There are ten or more people in this town, or not far away, of world class, including my friends of abstract persuasion. In fact I think there is a substantial School of London ... If some of the strange and fascinating personalities you may encounter here were given a fraction of the internationalist attention and encouragement reserved in this barren time for provincial and orthodox vanguardism, a School of London might be more real than the onc I have construed in my head.[36]

Auerbach admired *The Family* and brought Wonnacott's work to the attention of Geoffrey Parton, who worked at Marlborough Fine Art: so he was taken on by Marlborough, then the most reputable, as well as the most commercial, of the Bond Street dealers, with its strong representation of School of London artists.

Wonnacott's career at the Marlborough was launched by his first exhibition in November 1980 and was widely reviewed (commercial exhibitions received much more attention than they do now). *The Family* was shown again. As William Feaver described it in the *Observer*:

> The most startling demonstration of his cinematic outlook is *The Family*, a huge composition that took him from 1963 to 1974 to get right. During that period it doubled in size and, besides being extended to wrap-around proportions, it increased in complexity to become a family saga, a dance to the music of time in an Essex back garden. The painting celebrates passing generations. The various members of the family each appear more than once, roles changing as they grow up and age. An apple tree casts all-embracing shadows over the company past and present.[37]

Marina Vaizey was likewise very admiring of what Wonnacott was trying to do – the ambiguities of his response to his subject matter, both highly analytical and dispassionate, but also, simultaneously, about the dynamics of family life – in the *Sunday Times*:

> It seems to me that Wonnacott ... is doing something new in figurative art. The highly structured, even geometric and mathematical compositions underpin the free play of emotions. These paintings are both restrained and highly charged with feelings.[38]

The Family is a big painting – big in ambition, a demonstration that Wonnacott expected to be taken seriously as a major painter working adventurously in the Slade tradition.

Chapter 4

Chalkwell

It is impossible to understand Wonnacott's career and the way that he has operated on the edge of the art world, away from its more international aspect, without paying attention to the fact that it has been embedded in a seaside community in Essex, the least fashionable of English counties, in a milieu of walks on the beach, cockles and mudflats.

Wonnacott bought a house high up on the riverfront above Chalkwell railway station. He describes how he chose the house because of the view out of an upstairs bedroom, which he has used ever since as his studio:

> Because that landscape was not just beautiful, but is my childhood. I was brought up in the London suburbs, but I had a granny who lived just round the corner from here, my grandfather worked a pleasure boat from that beach. I know that estuary. I used to walk out over that mud, those creeks, those rivulets. I know all those strange greeny-purply-greys of the mud, they are as deep a part of my childhood memories as the people that I loved.[39]

From his studio window, Wonnacott can survey, day in, day out, a broad view over the street – his friends and neighbours who wave up at him as they pass – and the trees in the municipal parkland stretching down the hill towards the beach and boats on the Thames estuary, in the always changing weather conditions, a view of the wide sky and water which have been his subject matter, sometimes obsessively. Wonnacott's world view is dominated by his life in Chalkwell – crab from the local fishmonger, his wife Anne working as assistant governor in the local Borstal, his children playing on the beach and going to local schools.

In his third year at the Slade, he had moved out of his parents' house in Finchley to lodge in Liverpool Road with a group of fellow students, and from there to Leigh-on-Sea to concentrate on his painting. He entered *Elms and Trellis, Marine Parade* for the Wilson Steer prize at the Slade (fig.13). It was shown at the London Group exhibition in 1963 and bought by the Ministry of Works for what became the Government Art Collection.

There are two early self-portraits made just after he had left the Slade. The first is an intense and highly experimental image of

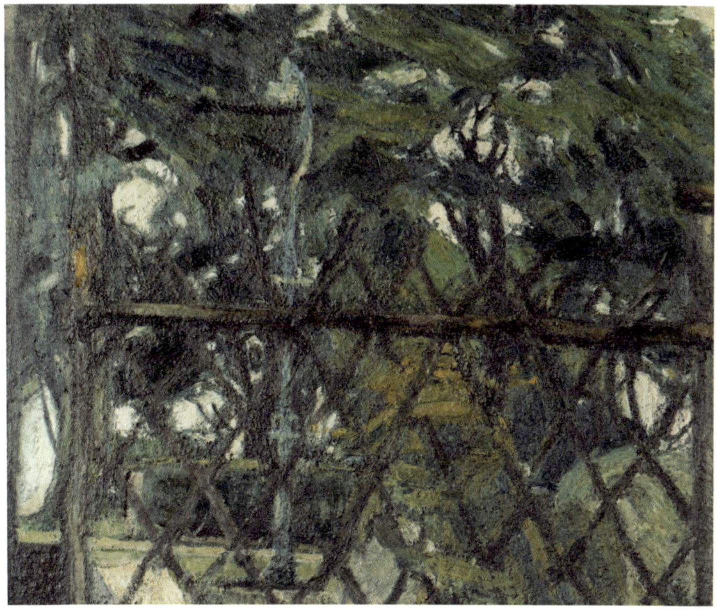

13. *Elms and Trellis, Marine Parade*, 1962

himself staring out wide-eyed from a background which is more like the inside of a fish tank than a room (fig.14). The other is a picture of a picture of himself under a naked light bulb, young and self-confident, a portrait within a portrait, a self-consciously distancing device, with a nod to Velázquez (fig.15). As Richard Cork writes in the introductory essay to an exhibition at the Yale Center for British Art in 2000:

> Staring at his reflection in a tall mirror, with brush in hand ready to apply another mark, he looks decisive. But the painting took seven years to complete. Wonnacott was, at this early stage, an unusually slow worker. Perhaps he felt inhibited by the achievement of Francis Bacon, whose influence can be felt in the naked light bulb shining down on a figure marooned in an otherwise deserted room.[40]

Wonnacott's other works from this period were studies of the withdrawn personality of his grandfather. In 1967–9, he began a study of his grandfather sitting in an armchair, which was subsequently bought from Marlborough Fine Art by Elaine and Melvin Merians, collectors from Larchmont, New York, who

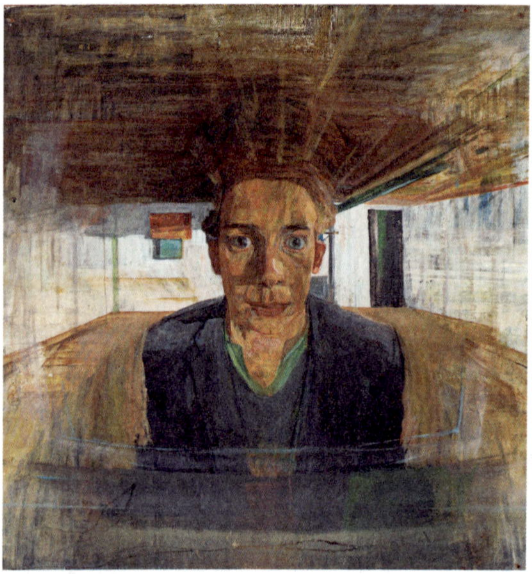

14. *Small Self-Portrait*, 1963–5

concentrated on building a collection by School of London painters, befriended Wonnacott and supported him over a long period (fig.16). Wonnacott described the importance of this picture in a letter he wrote to the Merians:

> 'The Grandfather' is one of a trio of large autobiographical pictures, all containing portraits of my Grandfather at the end of his life, that formed the nucleus of my work from my final year at the Slade in 1963 until I began exhibiting in 1972. For me, unlike most of my contemporaries in the 1960s, it was through the battle with appearances that painting offered its richest excitements, and this led to an intellectual fascination with problems of optical perception.[41]

In 1972, he met his future wife, Anne Wesolowska, and painted a number of pictures of her, most particularly a very beautiful one of her lying in the front garden of his parents' house in Marine Parade, Leigh-on-Sea. There are preparatory sketches and the finished painting is a confident and mature composition (fig.17): Anne fast asleep on the lawn, the privet hedges, the aeroplane flying overhead, the park in the distance, the sense of a hot summer. It is a fine work, with a sense that in the perimeter between the town and the estuary, he had found his subject.

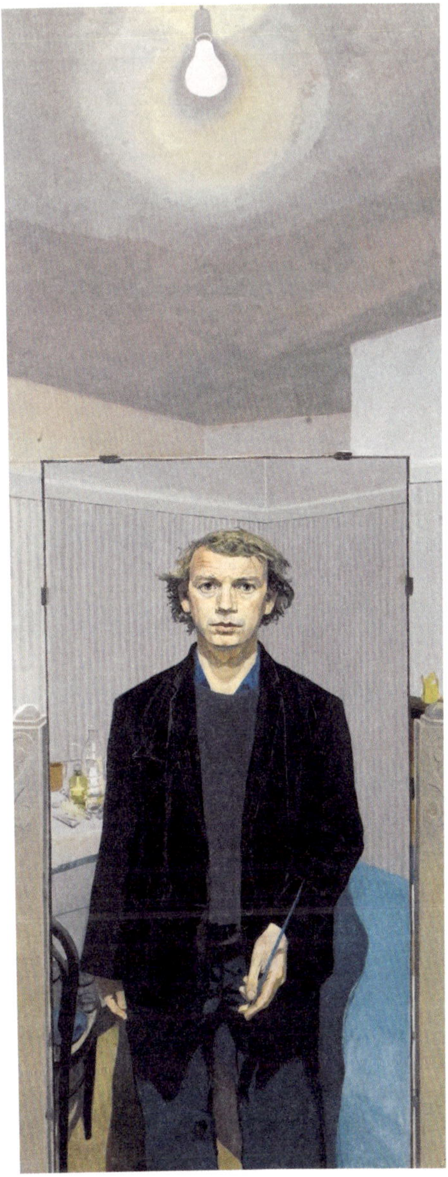

15. *Self-Portrait with Electric Light Bulb*, 1964–71

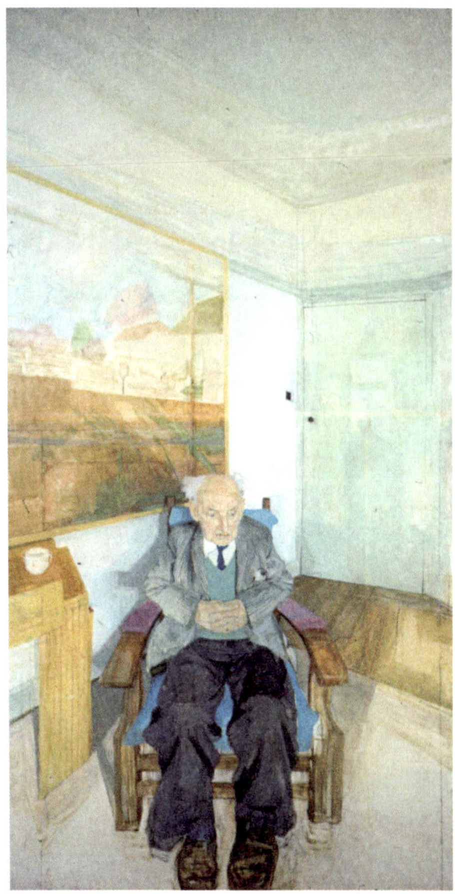

16. *The Grandfather*, 1967–9

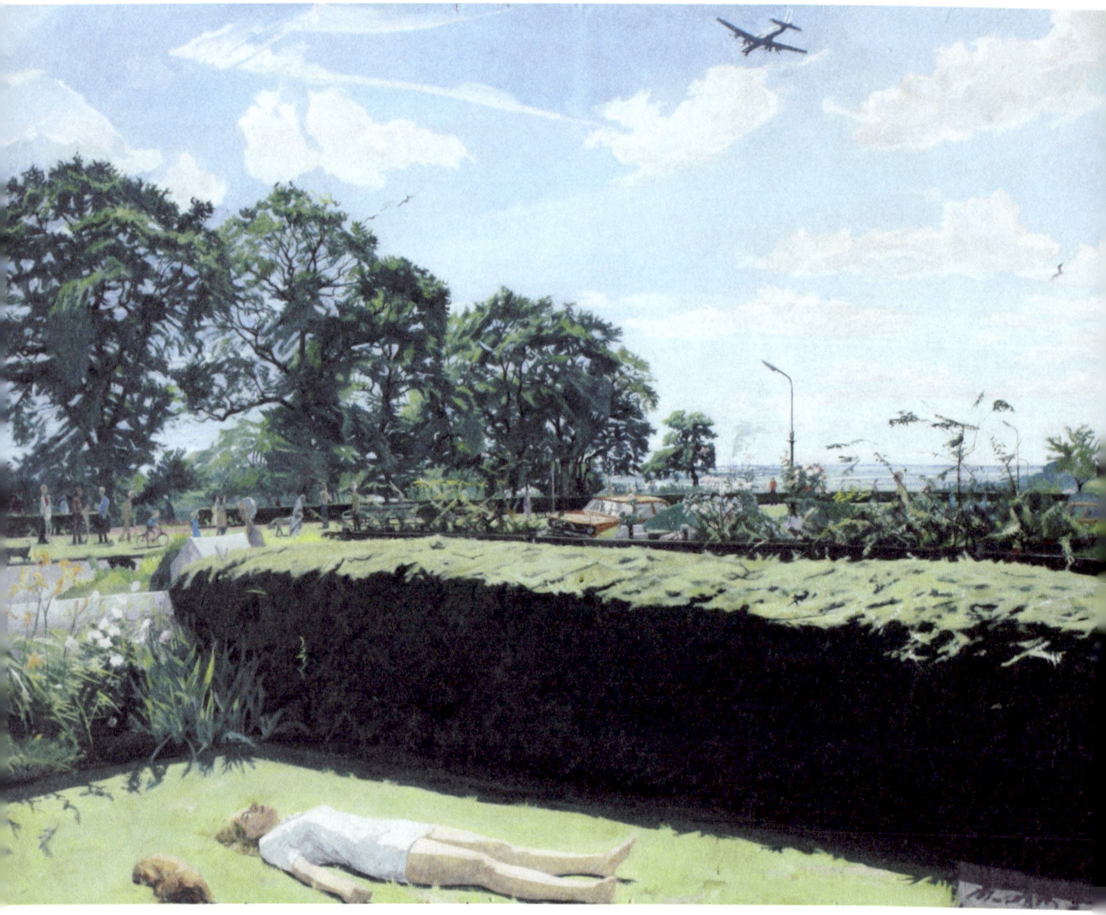

17. *Trees on Marine Parade with Anne Sleeping*, 1972–4

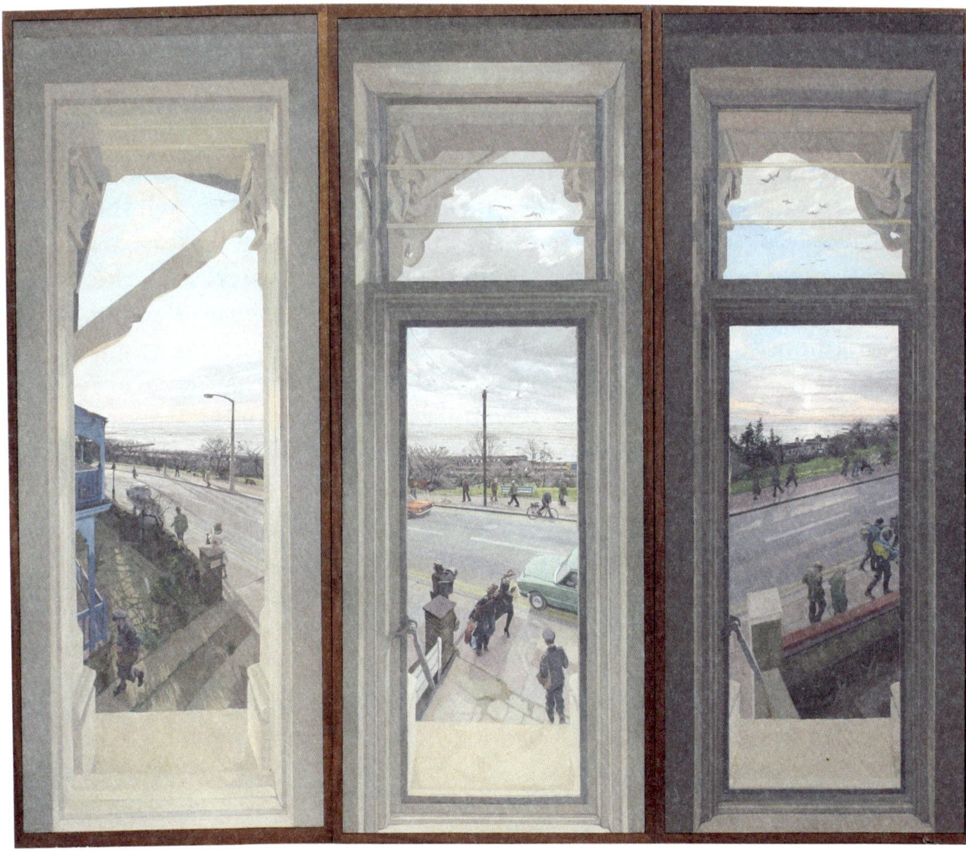

18. *Three Estuary Windows*, 1977–80

Having completed *The Family* in 1974, he began painting scenes from Chalkwell: a goat in the park leading down to the riverfront (fig.19); and *Estuary, the Steps* (fig.20).

In his first exhibition at Marlborough in 1980, Wonnacott included a series of tall paintings of the outside world as seen through the windows of his studio, ways of showing the changing seasons, as if they were scenes from Breughel (fig.18). His interest in the observation of everyday suburban scenery was unfashionable then and more so now, not least because these works were as much about the science of observation and perspective as they were about what was being depicted: getting the observer to think about the analytical procedure of depiction, the way that the eye works through vision. In reviews of the exhibition, critics struggled to define the nature and character of Wonnacott's attitude to the landscape tradition – he is not at all interested in the character of a landscape, which is in some ways wilfully nondescript, just a view out of what was an upstairs bedroom window onto the street and the scene below. The image is about the nature of perception, the optics of how the world is seen, not *what* is seen. As William Feaver wrote in the *Observer*, making clear his admiration for what Wonnacott was trying to do:

> Wonnacott has taken to painting the view through the window in series: high tide, low tide, morning, noon and night, all the year round ... Though the artist records the comings and goings of the people of Leigh-on-Sea – the train pulling in, commuters making a dash for it, the postman, the afternoon surge of OAPs, and holidaymakers in season – his overriding concern is the state of the light. The estuary empties and refills, rain sets in from the west, spitting on the right hand window pane. When darkness comes, navigation lights fizzle in midstream and refineries become beacons over the water. Wonnacott's preoccupation is perceptual accuracy: the way our paired eyes take in surroundings, focusing on what we single out for attention, but simultaneously sensing a great deal more across an almost 180 degree arc.[42]

Marina Vaizey wrote in the *Sunday Times* how 'these paintings, which are touchingly awkward, almost graceless in their patient

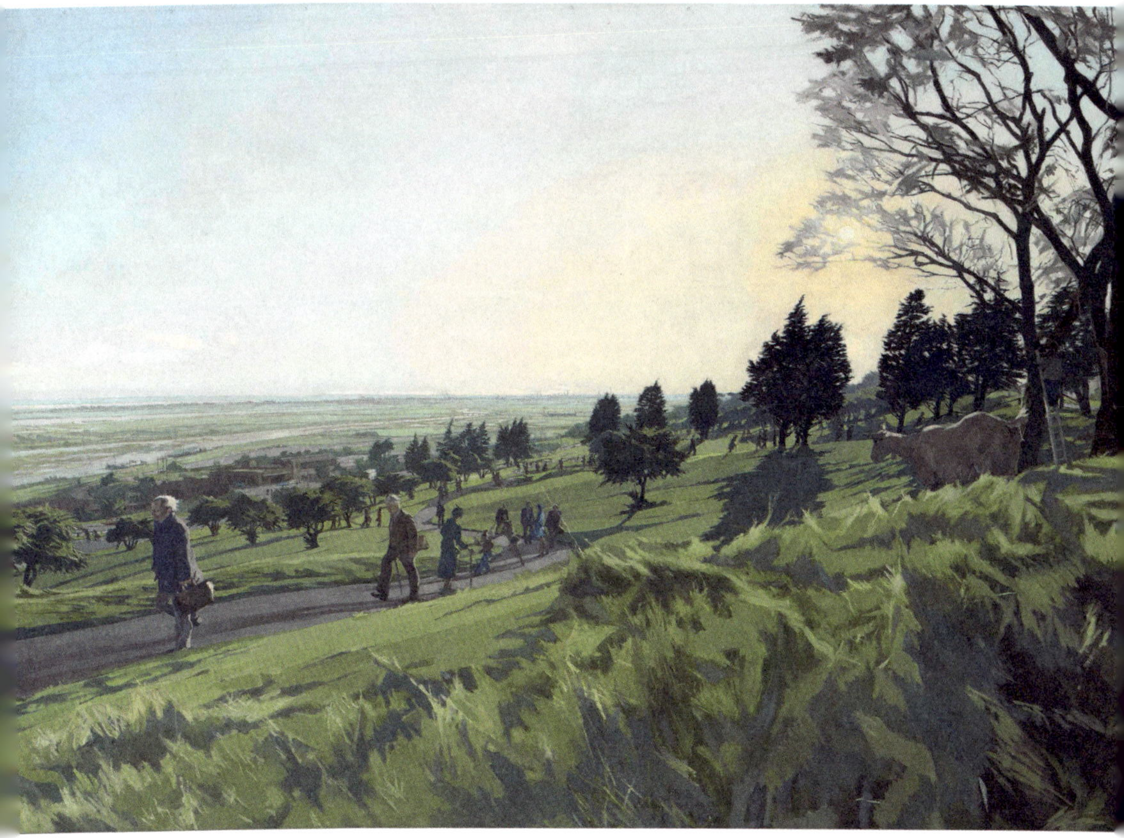

19. *Estuary, the Goat*, 1976–8

Overleaf
20. *Estuary, the Steps*, 1976–7

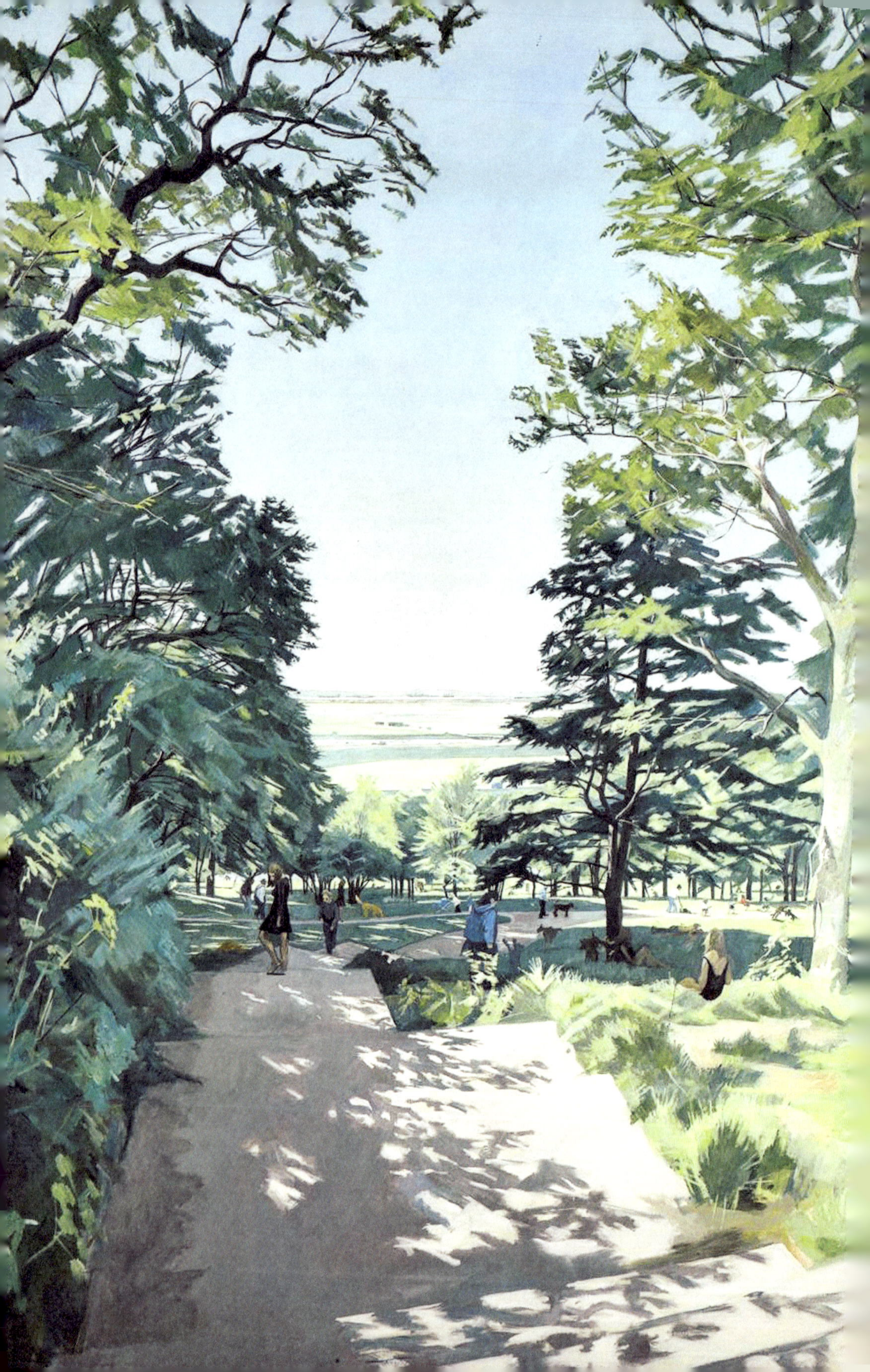

sincerity, combine a lively sense of spontaneous observation and that sense of contrivance that borders on the theatrical'.[43] This is a very good description of Wonnacott's virtues both then and since: painfully won imagery, neither purely naturalistic, certainly not super-realistic, as was fashionable at the time, but somehow intense redefinitions, re-descriptions, reimaginings of the ordinary, everyday seaside world, perhaps closest conceptually to the work of Stanley Spencer or Edward Hopper.

It is interesting to think about the artistic precedents for these paintings. There is, of course, a long and honourable tradition of British landscape painting, although in the period since the Second World War, it has been much less prominent in the mainstream of British art practice. Patrick George painted drily observed landscapes in Suffolk when he was not teaching at the Slade, but these were paintings of trees and fields, more in the tradition of Rubens and Constable, although, like Wonnacott, deliberately not picturesque, as much about the process of study and observation. Michael Andrews, who was such an influence on John, was beginning to explore less obviously urban scenes through, for example, a picture based on a photograph of the pier at Great Yarmouth and, from 1975, views of the Scottish Highlands, where he used to stay every summer with Jane Willoughby, a landowner, collector and close friend of Lucian Freud. In 1977, Andrews and his wife June moved out of London to the village of Geldeston, near Beccles in Suffolk, and then, in 1981, to Saxlingham Nethergate, south of Norwich. He is said to have wanted to paint scenes of 'mysterious conventionality':[44] in other words, demonstrating that even the most ordinary of urban or rural scenes has a type of visual interest to it; that it is not what is painted that is of interest, but how it's painted. John Virtue (born 1947), an artist at the Slade in the mid-1960s, the generation after Wonnacott, had moved back to Lancashire where he had been born, in order to paint the local landscape in the style of Samuel Palmer (1805–1881). And it should not be forgotten that 1975 was the year of the Brotherhood of Ruralists, which included the pop artist Peter Blake, who retreated to the village of Wellow in Somerset to paint the countryside in oil and watercolour.

But Wonnacott's attitude to painting the streets and municipal parkland in Essex is not imbued with an idea of rural idyll or English nostalgia. He is a realist, painting what he sees, interested in issues of pure painting – the clouds as much as the streets, mudflats at least as much as sand, sea breaks stretching out from the shore, water and sky. If anything, his painting is anti-picturesque, a commemoration of the realities of the ordinary outside world, not a glorification of it. Chalkwell has no connotations of rural mystery. Wonnacott's paintings are about what is: realism, not ruralism.

Chapter 5

Teaching

Like most artists of his generation, Wonnacott went straight into teaching part-time as a way of making an income to support his work as an artist, beginning with a year at Norwich School of Art in 1964, replacing a wild figure, Ken Brazier (born 1933), who had been a close friend at the Slade (the two men were introduced by John Lessore and Brazier introduced Wonnacott to Lucian Freud).

From Norwich, Wonnacott moved to Reading University, which has its own school of art and where he was recruited by Claude Rogers, who had been appointed professor and had known Wonnacott since before he went to the Slade – indeed, had been instrumental in his admission there. Wonnacott taught alongside John Tancock, who had studied art history at Cambridge and took him to Covent Garden to see Rudolf Nureyev and Margot Fonteyn dance. They used to meet for tea in the common room, together with Frank Bowling, who was also teaching part-time. Wonnacott ran the life room with his admired friend, the painter Ray Atkins (born 1937).

In the early 1970s, Wonnacott taught at his local art school in Southend and at Epsom. From here, he moved back in September 1976 to teach again at Norwich School of Art, where Edward Middleditch (1923–1987), a traditional figurative painter who had exhibited at the Beaux Arts Gallery, had been appointed Head of Fine Art in 1974 and had decided, following *The Human Clay* exhibition at the Hayward Gallery, to resurrect the school's life room. According to Lynda Morris, who was Gallery Curator and taught art history there from 1980:

> The large ground-floor riverside studio had the most beautiful quality of perfect north-facing light on the banks of the River Wensum. There were Victorian plaster casts of *Apollo*, a reclining River God, the *Discophorus* and the *Venus de Milo* lining the walls. There was a full-length plastic skeleton, anatomy charts of the skeleton and the musculature, and reproductions of figure drawings by Van Gogh and Seurat. The model was posed at the far end and there were about a dozen students working at easels on paintings and sight-size drawings.[45]

Writing from the perspective of the 21st century, the victory of an art which is based on its politics – the character of its ideas,

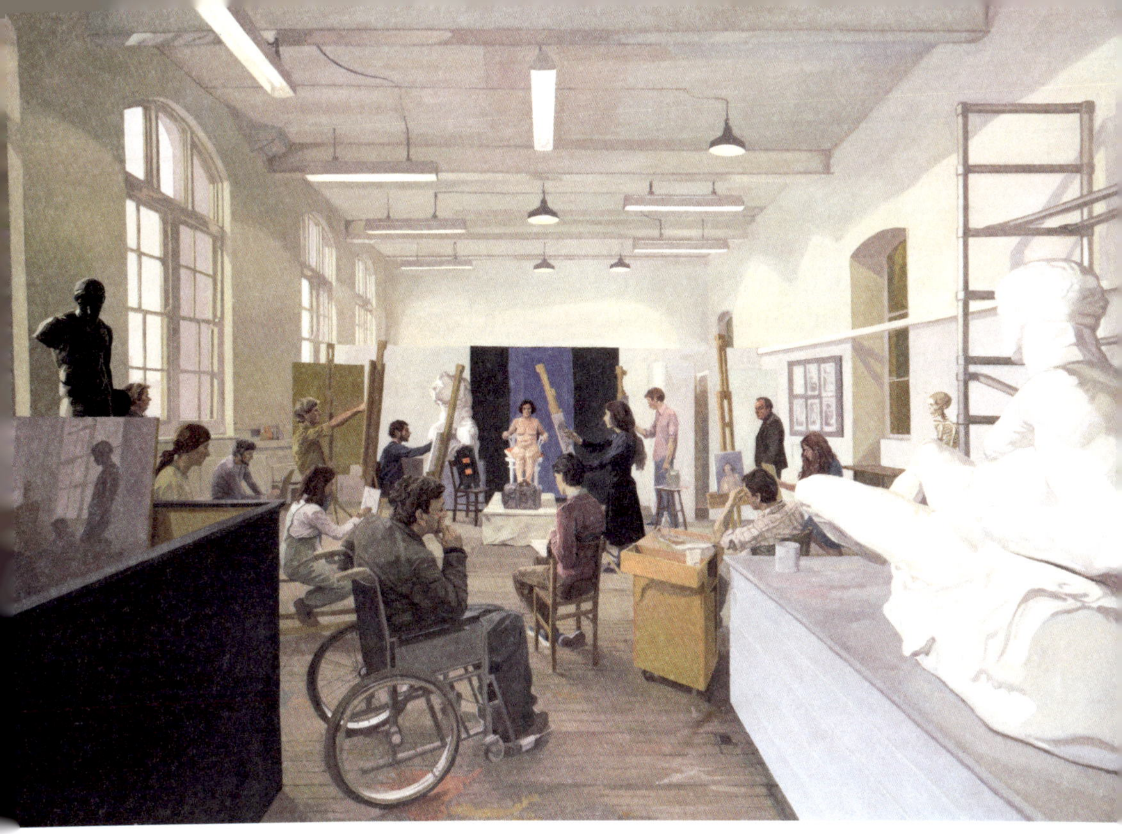

21. *The Life Room*, 1977–80

its belief in the essential characteristics of transgression and its commitment to 'the new' – looks inevitable. But in the late 1970s there had been a backlash against the avant-garde, led by artists like Kitaj and David Hockney (born 1937), rediscovering the pleasures and challenge of drawing from the model and the continuing legitimacy of painting within a long tradition.

In 1977, Wonnacott persuaded Middleditch to hire John Lessore to teach alongside him and together they formed a formidable pair in the life room, encouraging students to work from the model and to look at the techniques of Old Master painting, the traditions in which they had both been taught. According to Lynda Morris:

> The tutors made their own paintings alongside their students. John Lessore worked in a half-height alcove at the back of the studio on his painting of the model and John Wonnacott worked on the back wall on a large-scale painting.[46]

While at Norwich, Wonnacott painted a big picture of the life room (fig.21), which was shown in *John Wonnacott: First London Exhibition* at Marlborough Fine Art in late 1980 and was bought by the Norwich Castle Museum with help from the National Art Collections Fund (now the Art Fund). It is a fine picture, giving some idea of the intensity of the life room, the commitment of the students to this form of art practice, with Lessore sitting pensively in his wheelchair in the foreground and the geometry of the strip lighting above. As Marina Vaizey wrote in her review:

> At the end of a large room the naked, not quite young woman sits with dignity, raised on a dais. A lot of other people are in the light-filled, large white space; the teachers and the taught, and here and there, a skeleton, plaster casts.

She conveyed a sense of the originality of his approach: 'Wonnacott's paintings are intense, full of feeling, autobiographical, and accessible.'[47]

Lynda Morris describes the atmosphere of Norwich art school as it was in the 1980s:

> As with Coldstream, I was in the company of artists who had a moral authority. The whole school in the early 1980s still had a military aura. Technicians would virtually stand to attention when speaking to the Principal. Middleditch had been wounded in the Ardennes in fierce fighting and had won the Military Cross. Henderson was in the Air Force and was emotionally exhausted by bombing raids on Germany. He went to the Slade in 1945 to recover from a breakdown. Most of the older staff had at least done National Service. Decisions were seen as a matter of life and death. They had little time for the Academic Board but immense time for the next generation, for their students.[48]

For his next exhibition at Marlborough in 1985, Wonnacott painted a portrait of Lynda Morris, cigarette in hand, one of his first exercises in pure portraiture, a picture that Kitaj much admired (fig.22). He also worked on two large paintings, which he painted in full view of the students at either end of the life room.

22. *Lynda*, 1982–4

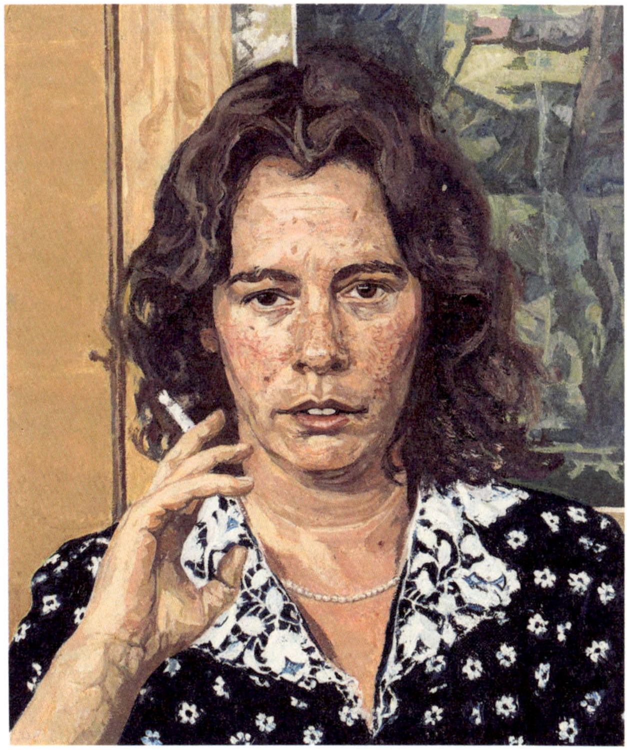

He remembers 'what a challenge it was to paint both canvases in full view, in front of his students, and how valuable it was to train himself to work under the threat of constant interruption'.[49]

The first of these was a view of Norwich Cathedral (fig.23), a big, ambitious civic picture, looking as if it was painted in the 1950s rather than the 1970s, with the bishop advancing towards the spectator and the dean and chapter assembled by the west front of the cathedral in an arrangement that echoes the asymmetry of the building's facade.

The second was of the dark, red-brick building of Norwich School of Art – originally built as the City of Norwich Technical Institute between 1899 and 1901 – seen from Blackfriars Bridge across the River Wensum (fig.24). Shown in the Royal Academy's Summer Exhibition in 1984, it was bought by the Trustees of the Chantrey Bequest, and, long before the Summer Exhibition closed, transferred to the Tate so that it could be included in its exhibition, *The Hard-Won Image*, from July to September that year. Wonnacott describes its subject matter:

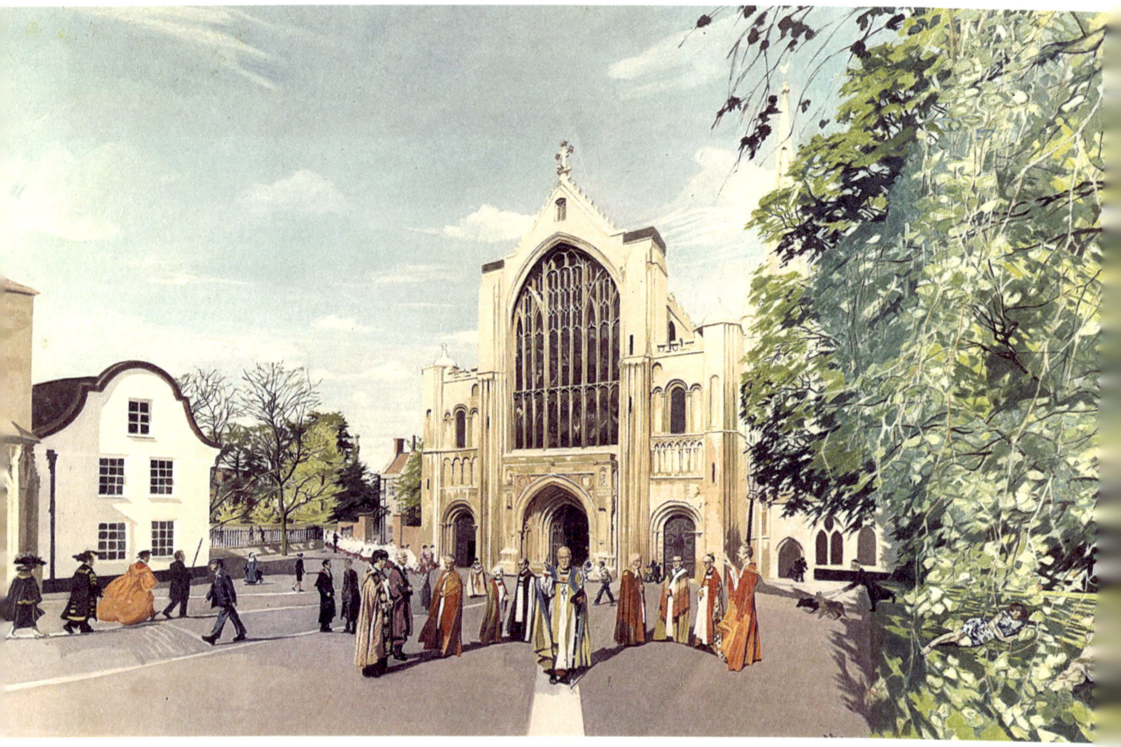

23. *Norwich Cathedral*, 1981–5

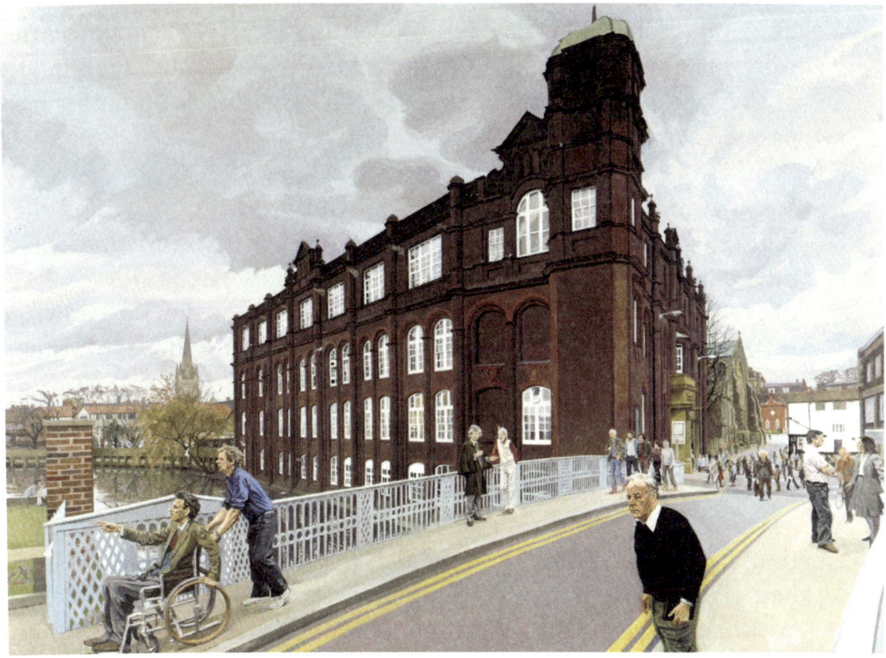

24. *Norwich School of Art*, 1982–4

> The red-brick facade with which the Norwich School of Art fronts the river and St George Street forms the subject of my second large portrait of a Norwich building. From the hierarchy of Art School figures stretched between the pubs at either end of [St] George Street, a double portrait of John Lessore and myself is seen walking, in parallel to the central figure of Edward Middleditch, out of the painting to the left. Lynda Morris and Colin Tester (subjects for my two small portraits) are in conversation to complete the foreground triangle, on the far right of the painting.[50]

This was a painting with numerous surviving preparatory drawings of the setting. Wonnacott would go out at seven o'clock in the morning to draw, much preferring to rely on drawings rather than photographs to get a good sense of the overall composition. He added the figures later. On the left-hand side, as Wonnacott describes above, the artist is shown pushing his friend John Lessore in his wheelchair. On the pavement on the right, Edward Middleditch appears dignified and solitary, carrying a copy of a book representing his love of 17th-century poetry, particularly the work of John Donne. To the right are Colin Tester, the technician at the school, and Lynda Morris, both of whom Wonnacott had painted separately.

It is a grand narrative painting, wildly out of fashion at the time, but, on the other hand, regarded as sufficiently important to be included in *The Hard-Won Image*, organised by Richard Morphet, the Deputy Keeper in the Modern Collection at the Tate. Owing to his very plural, eclectic and undogmatic interest in art, Morphet was described in Richard Shone's review of the exhibition as having 'long been known (and both praised and attacked) for the scrupulous and sympathetic attention he has lavished on works widely different in intention and effect'.[51] In 1981, Morphet had been asked to contribute an essay to the catalogue of an exhibition, *Les Réalismes, 1919–1939*, held at the Centre Pompidou, which had given him a more sympathetic interest in those artists, like Wonnacott, but also including Kossoff, Auerbach, Freud and Kitaj, who had a commitment to painting outside or against the mainstream of modernist practice.[52]

Wonnacott's *Norwich School of Art* is one of his major paintings, but also a record of his undoing at Norwich. The mood in the art school was turning against figurative practice, which was increasingly regarded as irrelevant. Middleditch retired in 1985. In the summer of 1986, Wonnacott and Lessore were dismissed on the grounds that the Fine Art Department was 'changing its approach to the activities in the life room'. Lessore describes the episode laconically:

> Our work in the life room was so successful that we were sacked in the end. We were the only teachers in the school with West End dealers – a recipe for disaster. We were, in fact, quite happy to be sacked. Ed would never have sacked us; our success impressed him but it happened after he left for the Royal Academy Schools. I believe the upper echelons were all subsequently sacked for sacking us.[53]

According to Wonnacott, his picture of Norwich School of Art shows its three principal figures deliberately walking away from the School of Art 'like an Expulsion from Paradise'.[54]

Chapter 6

Dealers

During the 1980s, Wonnacott had a successful relationship with Marlborough Fine Art, which showed exhibitions of his work every few years.

His second big one-man exhibition, in 1985, showed the full range of his work: views of Southend, including *The Foreshore Superintendent's Hut* (fig.25) and *The Ladies' Bowling Green* (fig.27). There was a big picture of the Palace Hotel above the riverfront at Southend (fig.26) which divided opinion among his friends. Francis Bacon apparently hated it. Lucian Freud wrote how much he admired it. John Russell Taylor, the critic in *The Times*, liked the exhibition as a whole: not so much the topographical views, which he called 'photorealism in all the less appealing senses of the term', but more for its views of the Thames estuary, describing how 'when he is rendering the changes of light and weather across the sandy flats he has an extraordinary feeling for that very English sort of glaring greyness or the flattening effect of dusty sunlight at mid-afternoon'.[55]

In 1988, Wonnacott had another exhibition at Marlborough. He was concentrating on views of the mudflats of the Thames estuary,

25. *The Foreshore Superintendent's Hut*, 1981–4

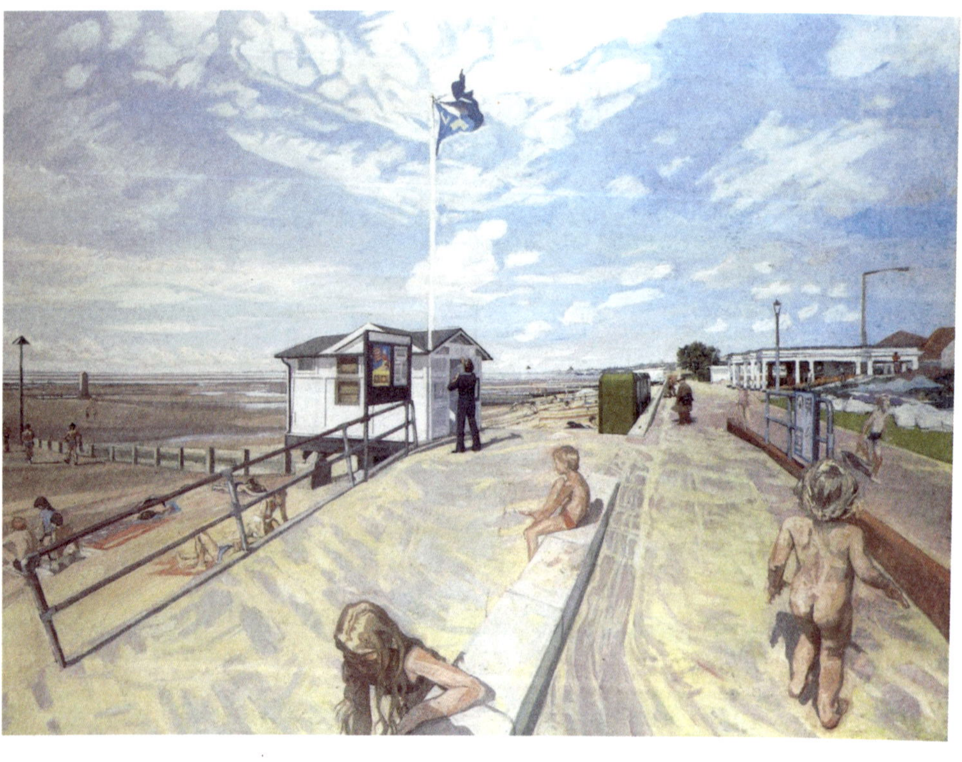

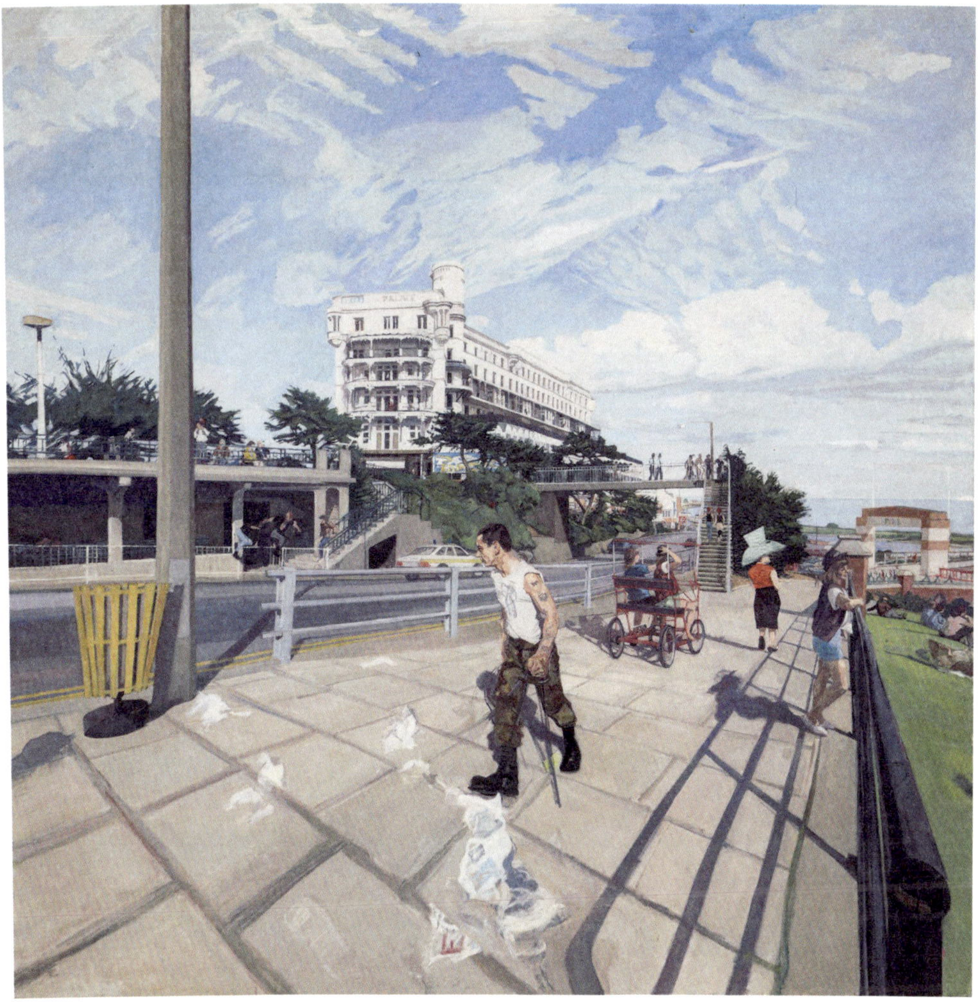

26. *The Palace Hotel, Southend*, 1983–97

beautiful wide, open expanses of sky and tide, with figures running or walking in the distance or children playing. They are the seaside as it is, unromanticised (figs 28, 29, 30). Wonnacott described the nature and purpose of these paintings with unusual lyricism (he is a carefully observational painter, not a poetic one):

> The Estuary Mudflat pictures are built in the studio from drawings and photographs made in the few safe hours between tides on an intricacy of creeks at the end of the Chalkwell hard. Appearances there change with exhilarating speed and only

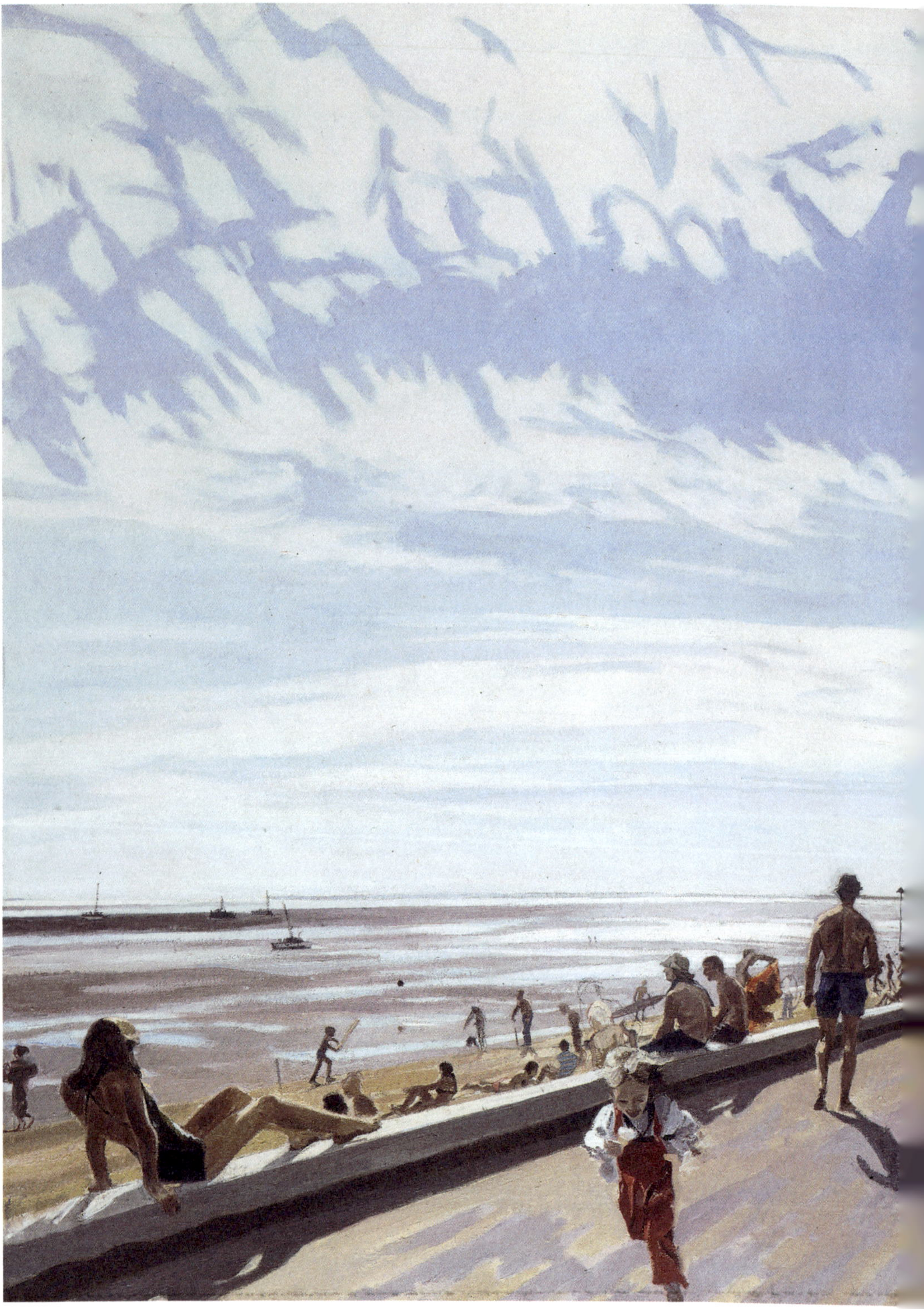

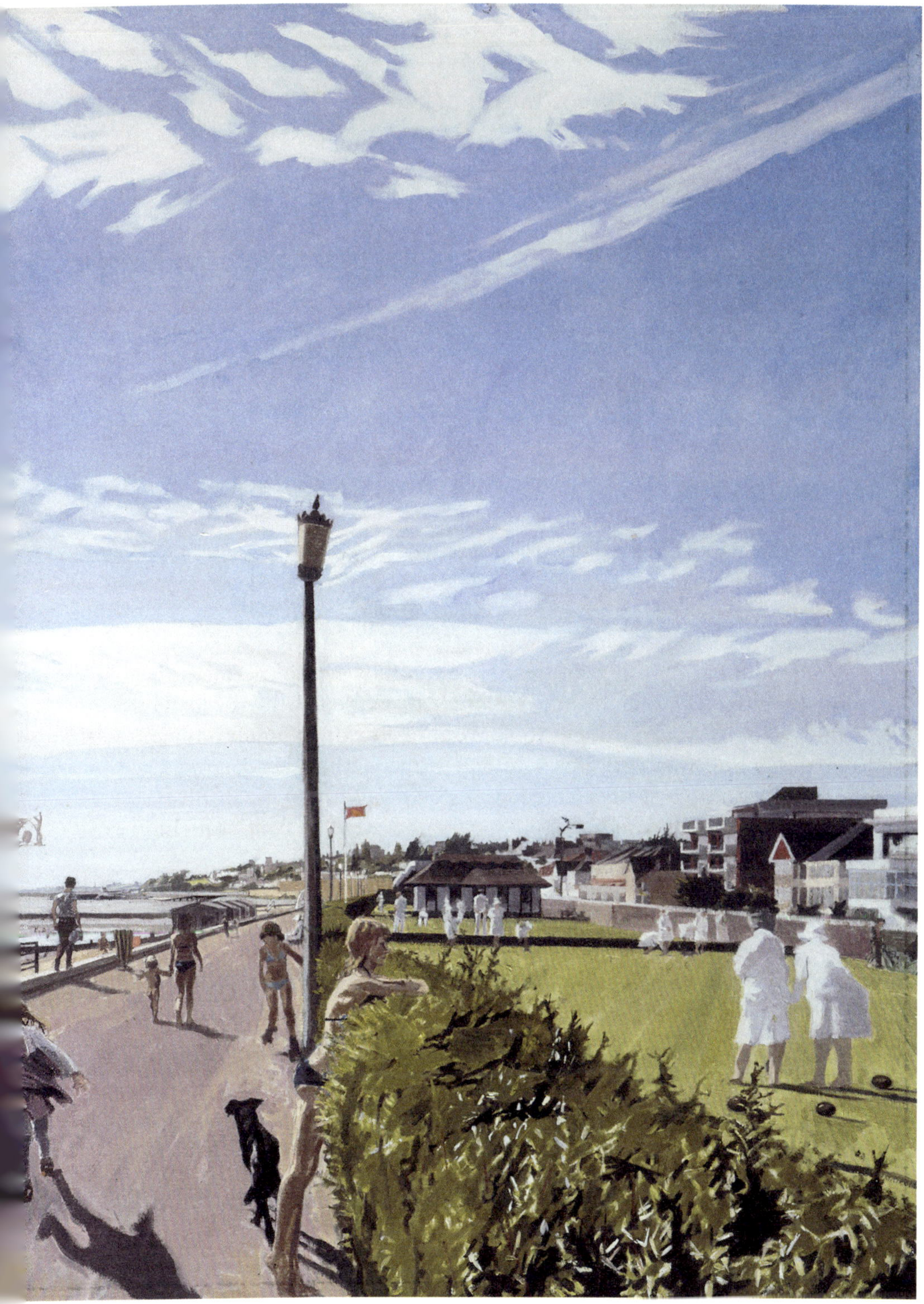

27. *The Ladies' Bowling Green*, 1981–5

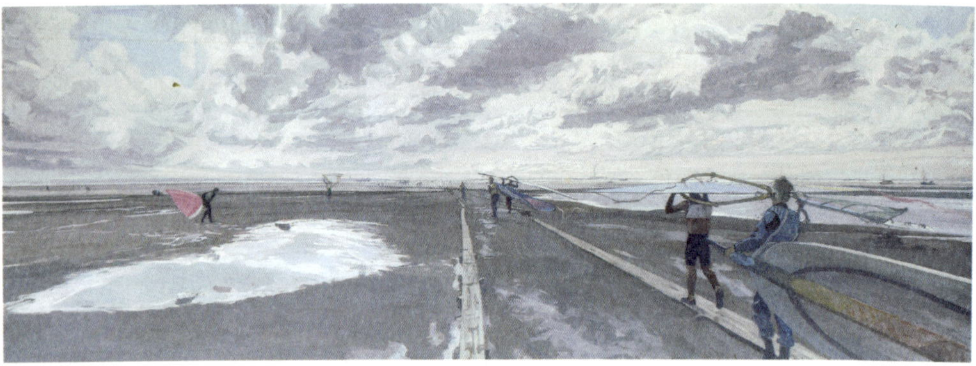

28. *The Hard*, 1985–8

> the horizon is built in to give formal stability. Near to the beach, shallow pools retain their low tide shaped formation for longer periods of study. Filled to their edges in reflected sky, they lie with the presence of great nudes stretched out across the horizontal field of vision.[56]

Unfortunately, paintings of the Essex mudflats are not perfect for the London, let alone the international, art market. Gilbert Lloyd, the owner of Marlborough, took Wonnacott out to lunch on his birthday and was very upset to learn that he had negotiated a commission from British Caledonian Airways without the involvement of Marlborough. What happened next is best told in Wonnacott's own words:

> At the end of the show, [Lloyd] told me at the post-mortem meeting that the sales were useless. With reference to the four golden mudflats, he explained to me, perhaps jokingly, that 'wealthy collectors didn't want to see poor children playing in the mud' ... Then, without the expected four-yearly top-up to my finances, I had to go to Geoffrey [Parton] cap in hand and ask for help. They came back with the offer to buy in four of my paintings for a quarter of their asking price. This wasn't unreasonable (today it would look like a miracle) but I was upset and as I had already decided to repaint one of the pictures, a 4 foot *Estuary Crowstone*, I explained this and rejected

their offer. Geoffrey came straight back and apologised, saying that they had already sold the picture I wanted to rework and it was too late to undo the contract. Still, I suppose fair enough, however annoying. Then on a visit to Fine Art Services, where Marlborough stored my pictures, I found my *Estuary Crowstone* waiting to be transported to the chairman's sister as a present. I didn't say anything but began putting out feelers towards a move. Very quickly Giles Auty came back to me to say that William Joll of Agnew's was interested. William came to Leigh and I liked him immediately – he had great charm. Without consulting Julian or anyone else, he offered me four times my annual Marlborough advance for a five-year as opposed to three-year contract.[57]

So Wonnacott moved from Marlborough Fine Art, at that time the safest of the mainstream international dealers on Albemarle Street, to Agnew's, which, at the time, still had a big reputation as a long-established Old Master dealer, with astonishingly grand premises between Bond Street and Albemarle Street, with acres of redundant space, laid out like a country house, and with a particularly beautiful top-lit gallery upstairs. William Joll was a cousin of the Agnews and the son of Evelyn Joll, then chairman of the firm, and had been encouraged to take on a small number of contemporary artists.

29. *Red Lifebelt, Chalkwell Beach, from the Promenade Looking to Kent*, 1990

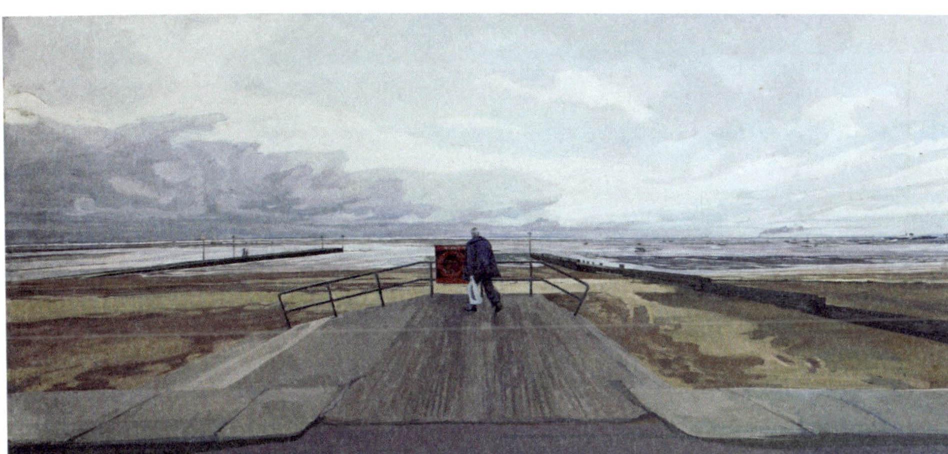

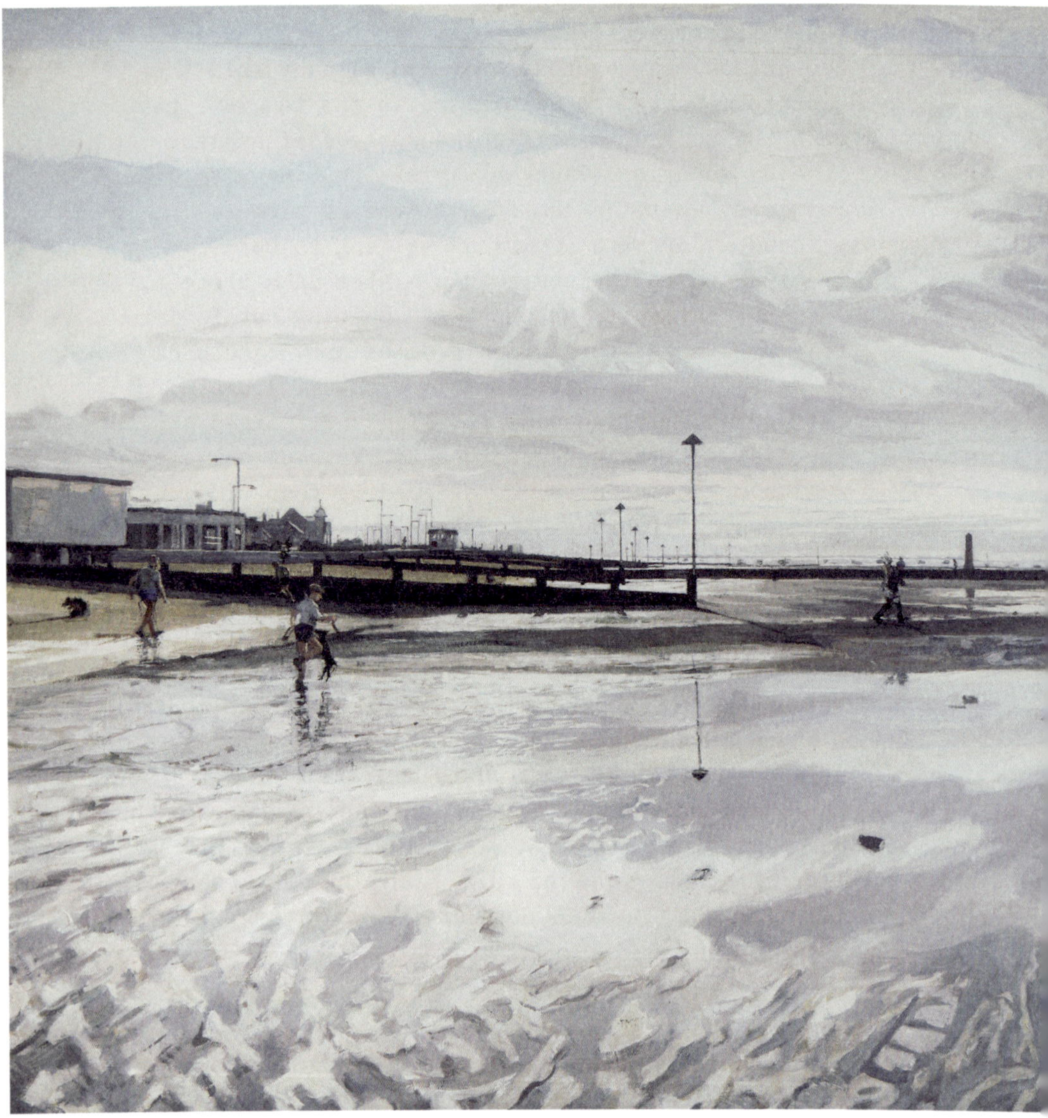

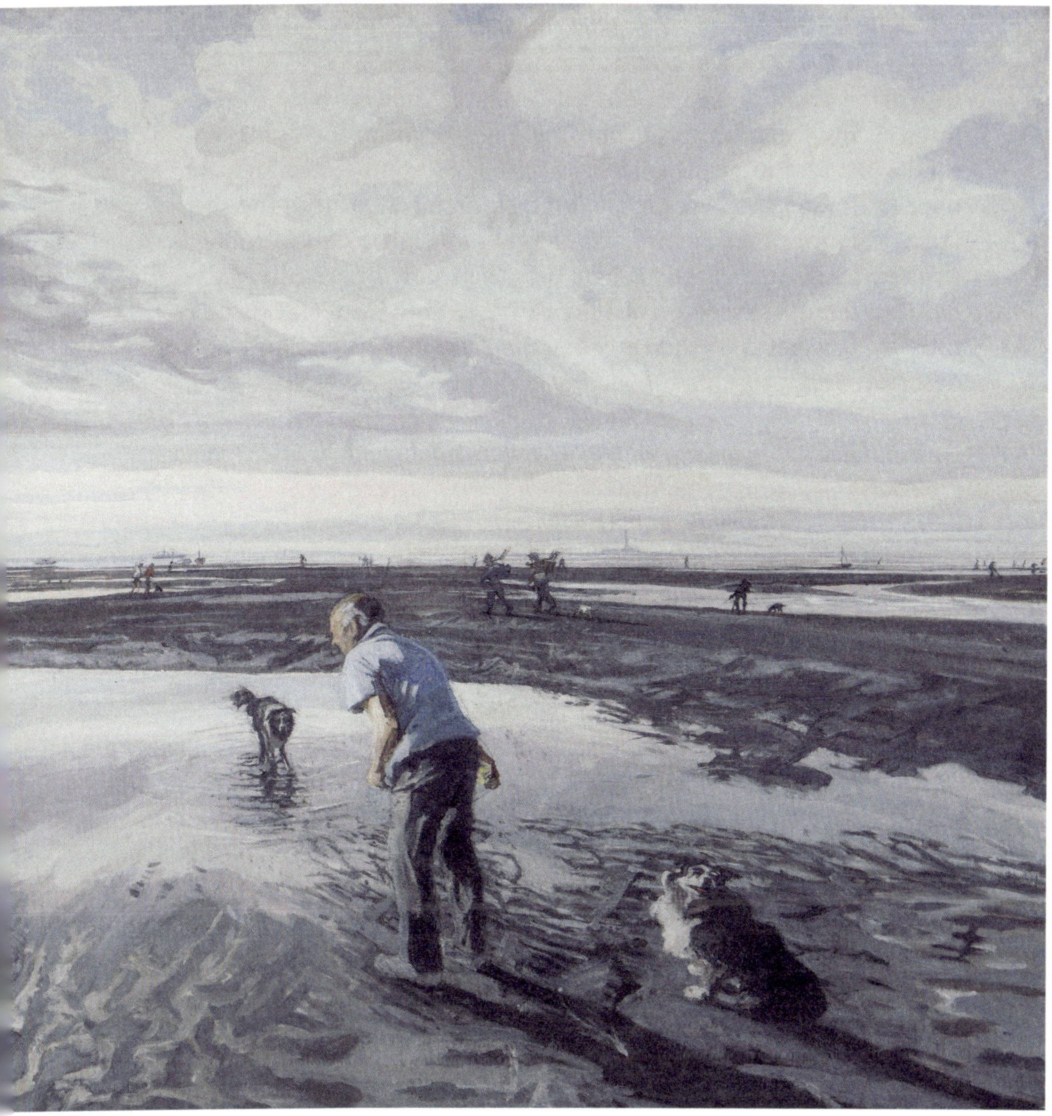

30. *Mud Pool with Collie*, 1985–8

Was this a good move or not? Wonnacott is still not sure. In the long term it probably was not, because Agnew's failed to make the transition from a traditional Old Master dealer with a secure international market to developing a new market for contemporary work and in 2008 sold its wonderful premises, which had opened in 1877, to Etro, the Italian fashion house. But in the short term, the move made sense. Wonnacott was more comfortable as a major figure in a gallery devoted to the tradition of Old Master painting than he had been trying to pretend that he was particularly sympathetic to the international avant-garde. Wonnacott describes the rationale for the move:

> The Agnew's galleries were vast and grand and I knew my pictures would look great there ... I loved the Jolls and the Kingzetts – they were like a world of connoisseur gents that had all but disappeared. ... In retrospect, and this is perhaps the most important reason of all, the negative client response to my last Marlborough show had shaken me. The world of Richard Hamilton, Michael Craig-Martin and White Cube was clearly in the ascendant (no interest at all in 'the discipline' of painting) and I could not see Wonnacott selling enough to support family and mortgage through the world of dealers.
>
> He [this is John referring to himself in the third person] wanted the negotiating freedom that Julian Agnew offered him to arrange his own commissions without reference to the gallery. This led to Wonnacott working over the next 20 years in some of the grandest spaces from Docks and Potteries to Palaces and Mansions. One commission a year provided a modest annual living that has enabled him to paint full-time on his beloved estuary.[58]

In 1992, Agnew's held the first of its exhibitions devoted to Wonnacott's work. Whereas paintings of Essex mudflats had looked out of place in Albemarle Street, they belonged comfortably in a gallery which had a long-standing commitment to English landscape painting – indeed, had first established itself in Manchester in 1817 as dealers to the 19th-century nouveaux riches, selling them the work of Constable and Turner. It included more of Wonnacott's wide, open views of the Thames estuary in different weather conditions, such as *Red Lifebelt, Chalkwell Beach, from the Promenade Looking to Kent* (fig.29) and *Chalkwell Beach, Floodwater Overflow, Late Afternoon* (fig.31).

The exhibition also included a series of self-portraits, one of which, *Night Portrait with Blue Easel* (fig.32), was bought in 1993 by the Metropolitan Museum in New York, on the recommendation of William Lieberman, a former curator at the Museum of Modern Art, who was chairman of the Metropolitan Museum's 20th-century department and had conservative interests in figurative art. Not long after, Wonnacott painted another view of his studio which showed him sitting late at night with two local friends, the painter and art teacher Ian Cox, in a striped shirt to the left, and the mathematician Bernard Neumann, in a checked shirt to the right. Also visible is Wonnacott's wife, Anne, reflected in the mirror behind the glazed doors (fig.33). This painting was bought by the Tate. These sales demonstrate how well regarded Wonnacott's work was at the time, being acquired by two of the most important international museums in the world just before the art world went through another of its periodic readjustments away from painting towards film, photography and sculpture and a new generation of artists, more likely trained at Goldsmith's than the Slade.

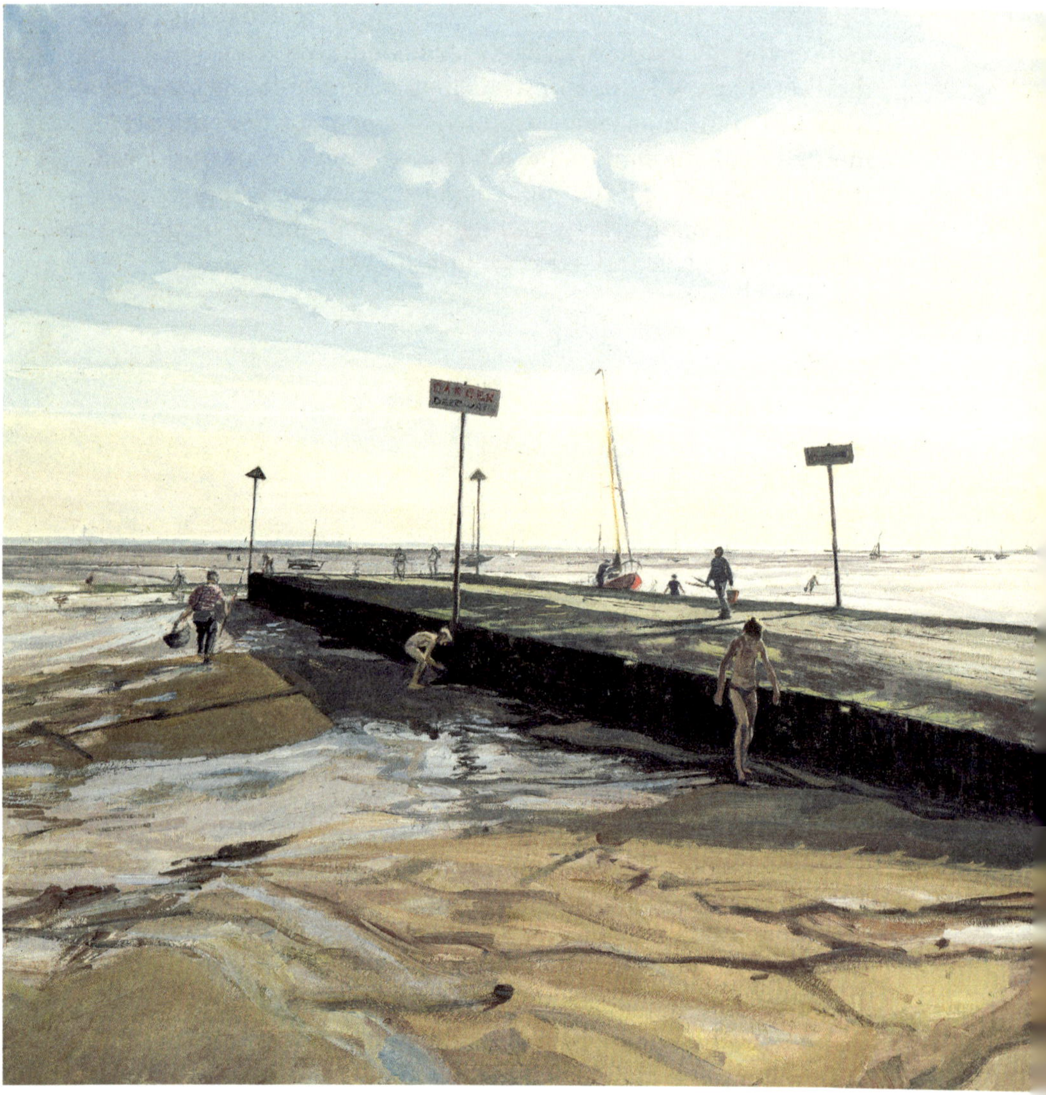

31. *Chalkwell Beach, Floodwater Overflow, Late Afternoon*, 1989–92

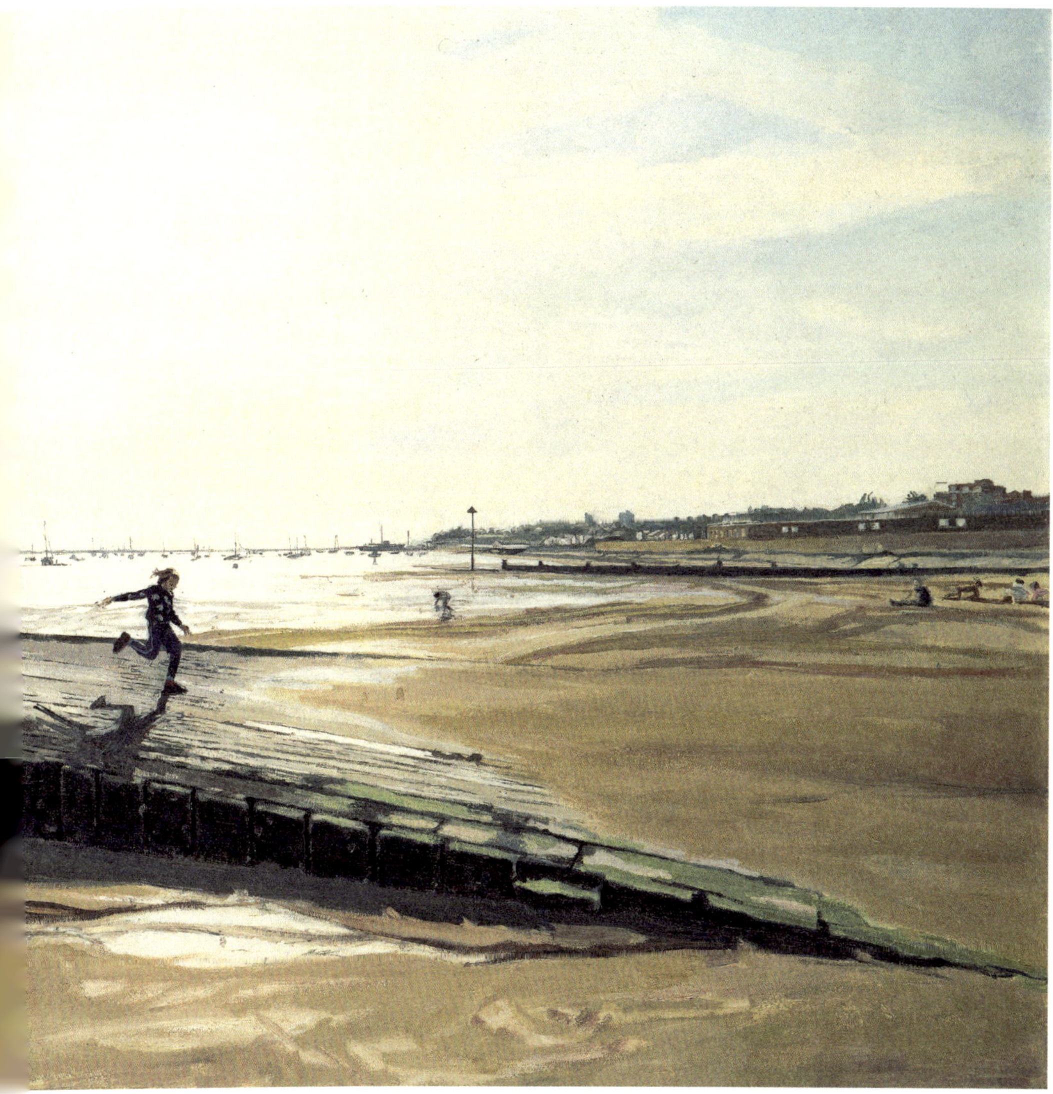

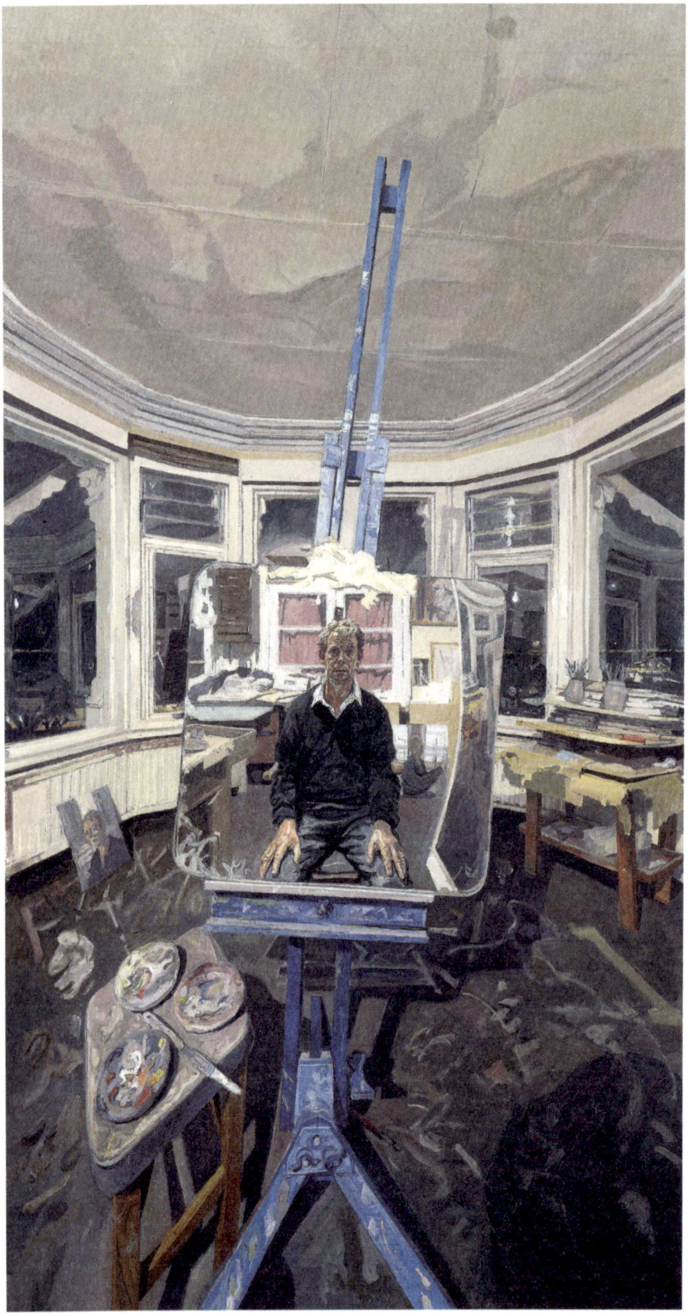

32. *Night Portrait with Blue Easel*, 1990–1

33. *Studio Conversation I*, 1993–4

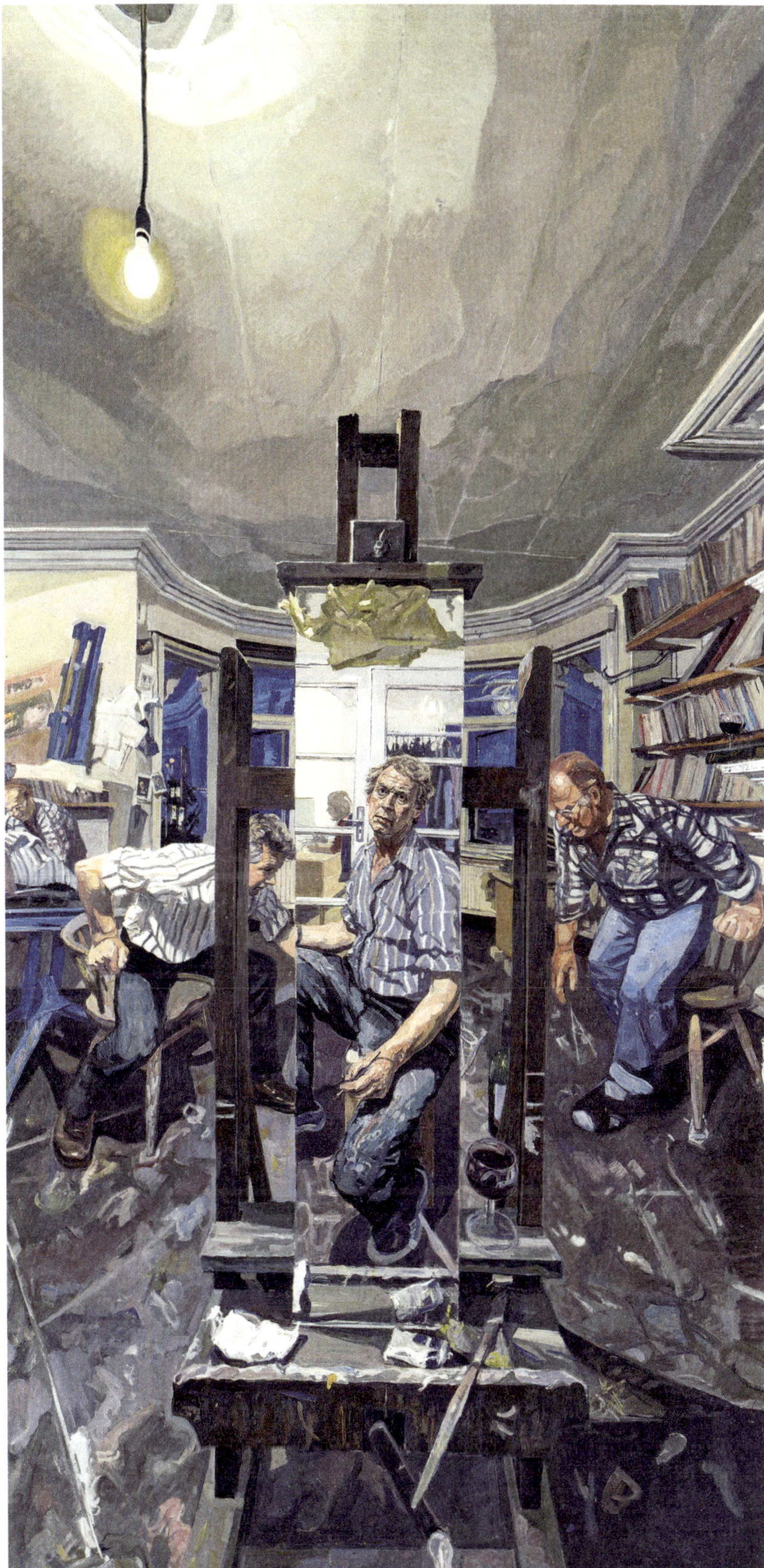

Chapter 7

John Major

When I arrived at the National Portrait Gallery as its Director in late January 1994, one of the tasks confronting me was to make sure that living prime ministers were represented in the permanent collection, if not by an available work which might be purchased, then by a commission by the Board of Trustees. Edward Heath was represented only by a fine but self-regarding photograph by Eve Arnold, taken in 1965 looking into a mirror shortly after he had become leader of the Conservative Party (NPG P521). I wrote to Heath and was summoned to meet him in his house in Wilton Street. He wanted to be painted by Lucian Freud. This was never going to be possible.

Next was what to do about John Major? In the mid-1990s, Major had a decidedly unglamorous public reputation: he was regarded by the press as second rate and always depicted by Steve Bell, the *Guardian*'s cartoonist, wearing his underpants over his trousers. On the other hand, he was still – but not necessarily for much longer – Prime Minister. We wanted to catch him while still in office, so that the portrait was not, so to speak, posthumous.

I am not sure who suggested John Wonnacott as the most appropriate artist to paint Major. It was most likely Robin Gibson, the Chief Curator, who admired Wonnacott's big portrait of Sir Adam Thomson, the founder of British Caledonian Airways, which Wonnacott had done as a commission for the Scottish National Portrait Gallery (fig.34). Thomson leans against the railing on the bridge of British Caledonian's hangar at Gatwick, a complex scene of men at work over which Thomson presides unautocratically. As Gibson wrote when he included the picture in his exhibition *Painting the Century* in 2000, where it hung between works by Jean-Michel Basquiat and Sonia Boyce: 'There are few enough paintings that deal with the facts and achievements of modern life, but Wonnacott's unique eye, sense of involvement and almost obsessive will to succeed have created one of its most remarkable manifestations.'[59]

I remember also that Henry Keswick, then Chairman of Trustees, endorsed the choice. He intuited, entirely correctly, that Wonnacott's style of social realism would be an appropriate match for John Major's unflashy, conscientious and down-to-earth ordinariness.

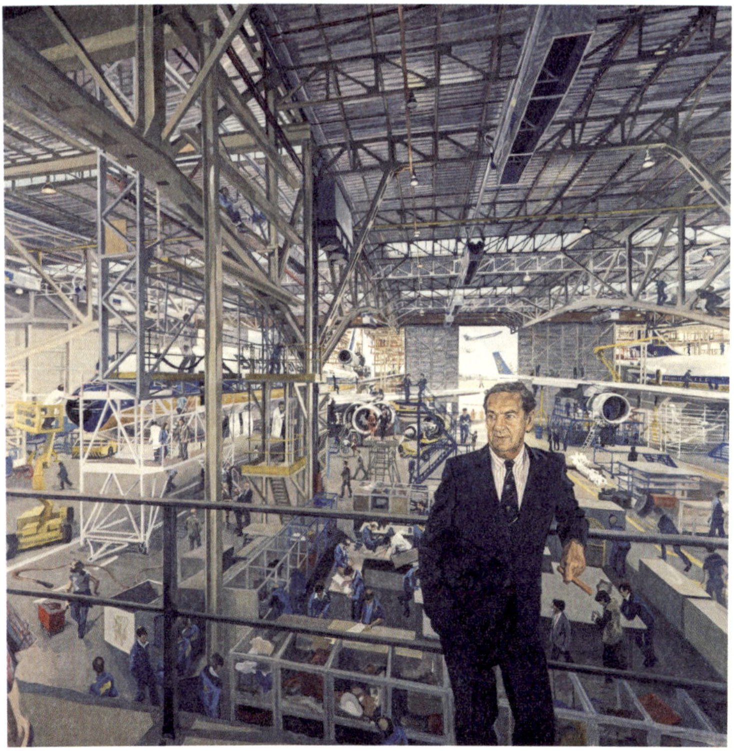

34. *Sir Adam Thomson*, 1985–6

35. *Study for John Major*, 1997

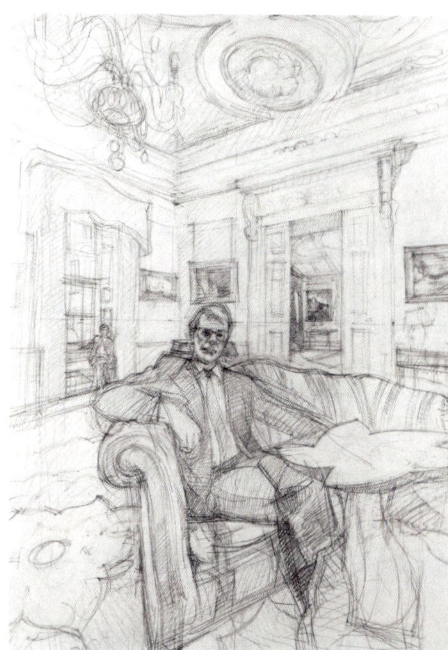

Overleaf
36. *The Rt. Hon. Sir John Major, Downing Street*, 1997

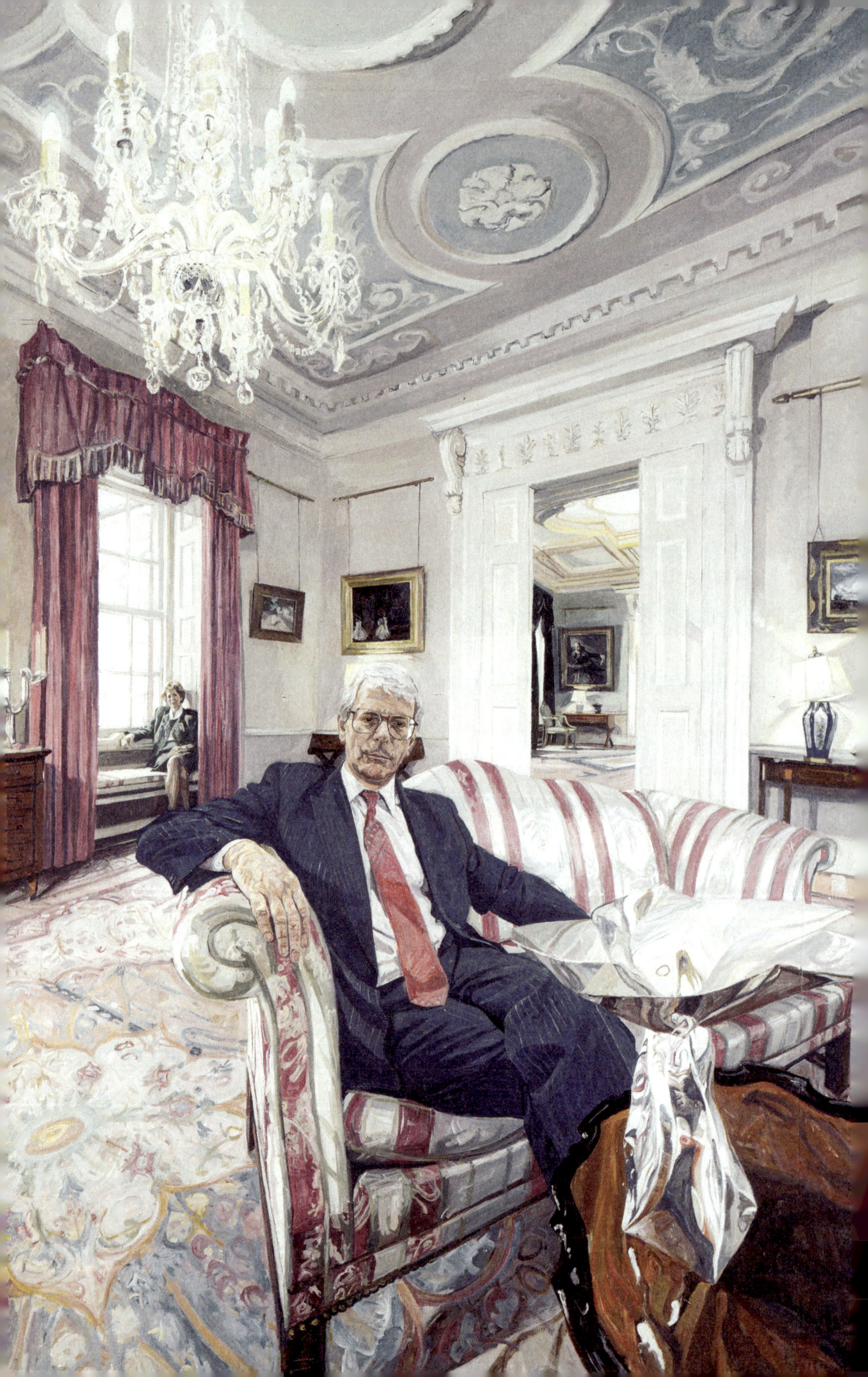

We negotiated sittings via John Holroyd, the Prime Minister's patronage secretary. Holroyd brought Major on a visit to the Portrait Gallery on one of his monthly recreational afternoons out of Downing Street to meet the people, when he made an unexpectedly good impression on everyone he encountered. He was much taller than he was depicted in the press, more commanding and straightforwardly friendly, not pretending to a deep knowledge of history, but intelligently interested in everything he was shown, including, most especially, individuals he met.

Wonnacott was allowed to work regularly in the White Drawing Room upstairs at 10 Downing Street over many months, drawing Major whenever he had half an hour to spare. But the painting was far from complete when Major lost the election catastrophically in May 1997. I remember thinking it was a pity that the portrait would show Major in the final stages of office when his authority had ebbed away, and there was something lugubrious about him sitting on a sofa surrounded by the appurtenances of power not long before his departure. The preparatory drawings (fig.35) show him preoccupied, his facial expression hidden behind over-large spectacles, with a look of anxious intensity that was very characteristic of him but was probably merely indicative of the troubles of high office.

So, the question was how and where was the portrait to be completed, once Major was out of Downing Street? Wonnacott wanted somewhere quiet where he could set up his easel. I never did find out how he discovered that there was a hut on the roof of the office wing of the National Portrait Gallery on Orange Street which he decided would suit him perfectly as a studio. He moved in for what I remember as a very long period when he would invite people to picnic lunches in the studio and got to know all the staff, especially the security team. A particular trait, and one that makes him a good portrait painter, is that he gets on with all sorts of people. John Major came to see the finished portrait. I walked with him into the upstairs room used for trustee meetings. It was full of contractors holding a meeting about the gallery's building project. They were surprised when the former Prime Minister walked in. John Major put them at their ease. Major and Wonnacott had some of the same characteristics: an admirable lack of self-importance, and a tendency to be underestimated for their skills, which they do not boast about.

I thought at the time – and still think – that Wonnacott's portrait of John Major is a remarkable work of effective pictorial record (fig.36). It is easy to think that this type of painting is straightforward. It is not. It is compositionally highly complex, built up from detailed studies, conveying personality and character with judicious authority, balancing a concentration on the sitter, his face nearly at the centre of the composition, with attention simultaneously on the setting, including Norma Major sitting observantly on the window seat in the background. Wonnacott's portrait of Major shows his strength as an artist, his ability to handle compositional complexity with ease, his interest in character and the relationship between sitter and setting. These skills do not earn an artist prestige nowadays. If anything, it is the other way round: they are regarded as attributes of documentary illustration, not of a work of art. Skill in visualisation and representation (they are not the same thing) is thought to be easily obtained, instead of being the result of a lifetime of looking, drawing, and thinking about what it is to look, draw and depict. Wonnacott is deeply interested, as well as deeply skilled, in the qualities and characteristics of depiction and how the best works of portraiture are informed by looking at, and analysing, art of the past. He works with a vocabulary of narrative invention.

Chapter 8

The Landscape of Essex

In the early 1990s, Wonnacott was commissioned by the National Trust Foundation for Art to paint the bleak landscape of Orford Ness, a peninsula off the coast of Suffolk south of Aldeburgh which had been acquired by the Ministry of Defence before the First World War to be used for secret experiments which led to the development of radar. After the war, it was used by the Atomic Weapons Research Establishment and, during the 1970s, by the Foreign Office as a base for the transmission of the BBC World Service. It is now a nature reserve, owned by the National Trust, accessible to the public only on occasional days to protect its rare shingle habitat. Wonnacott was

> bowled over by the surreal wildness of the place with its shingle paths across marshland, strewn with discarded ammunition, that linked the shingle covered earthwork laboratories that felt more like tombs from some ancient civilisation. This commission gave me three sessions of around three weeks each when I was ferried over to the island with easels, paints and provisions. I always included a crate or two of wine. There I had a caravan to live in and a jeep to drive around in, it was heaven. In those days I still used to drink quite a lot and it was great to roar around the Ness from lab to lab with bottle in hand.[60]

It was a perfect subject for Wonnacott, who relates to the elemental features of the East Anglian shoreline – the flat landscape, derelict industrial buildings and wide skies – which he depicts with his entirely unsentimental, quasi-documentary eye. He produced a set of big, important pictures which document the characteristics of this landscape, including *Shingle Laboratory No.1* (fig.37), *Shingle Laboratory No.2 with Orford Church and Castle* (fig.38), which was bought by the National Trust, following Wonnacott's exhibition at Agnew's in 1996 to be hung in its headquarters; *Shingle Laboratory No.3 with Lighthouse, Orford Ness*, which is owned by the Christchurch Mansion collection in Ipswich; and *Laboratory Pagodas Nos 4 & 5, Late Summer, Orford Ness* (fig.39). These pictures show his mastery of the post-industrial landscape. They were exhibited in Ipswich in 1998, in a show titled *John Wonnacott's East Anglian Coast*, organised by Rebecca Weaver, who had been his student at Norwich School of Art, with an exhibition catalogue including an

37. *Shingle Laboratory No.1*, 1994–6

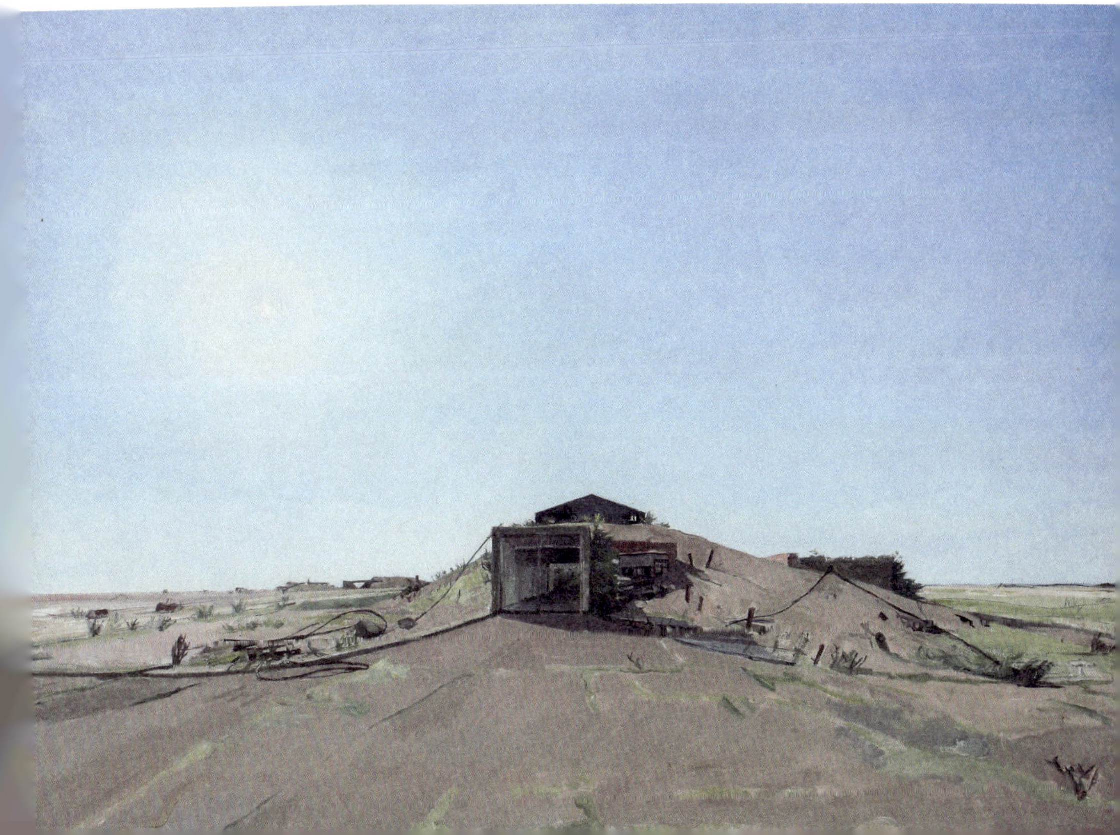

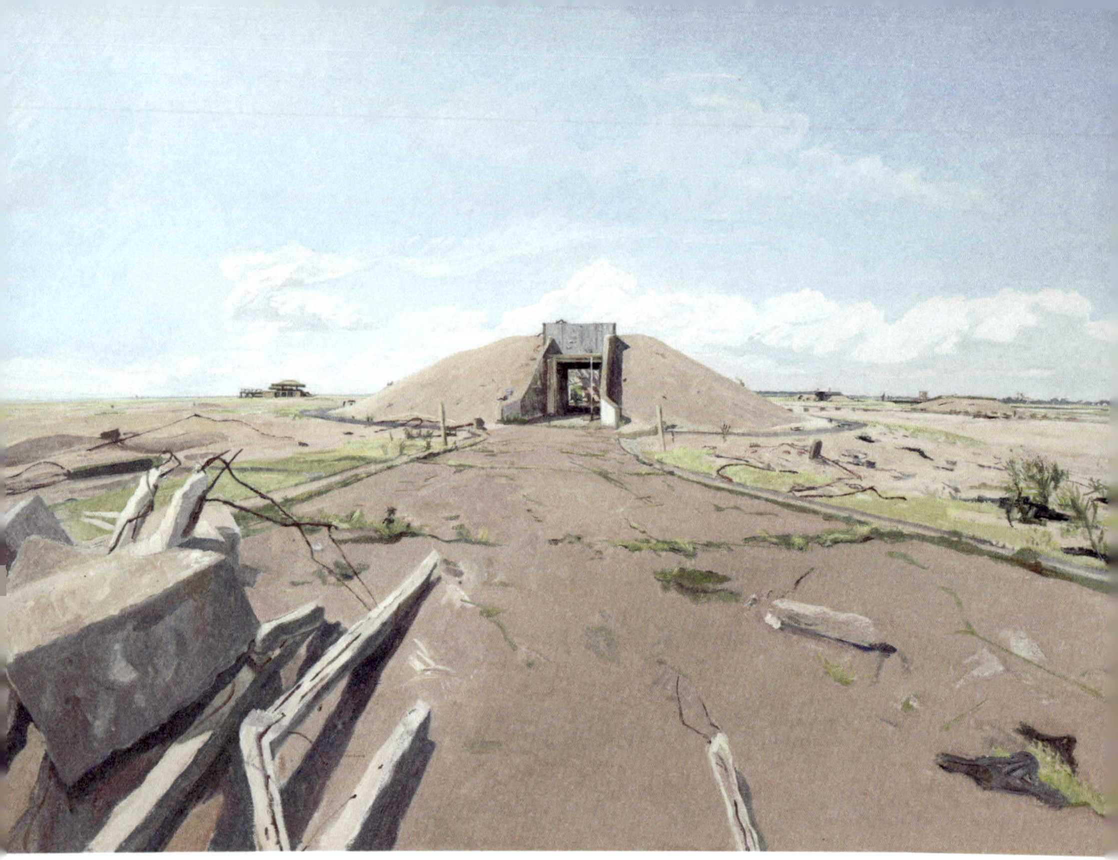

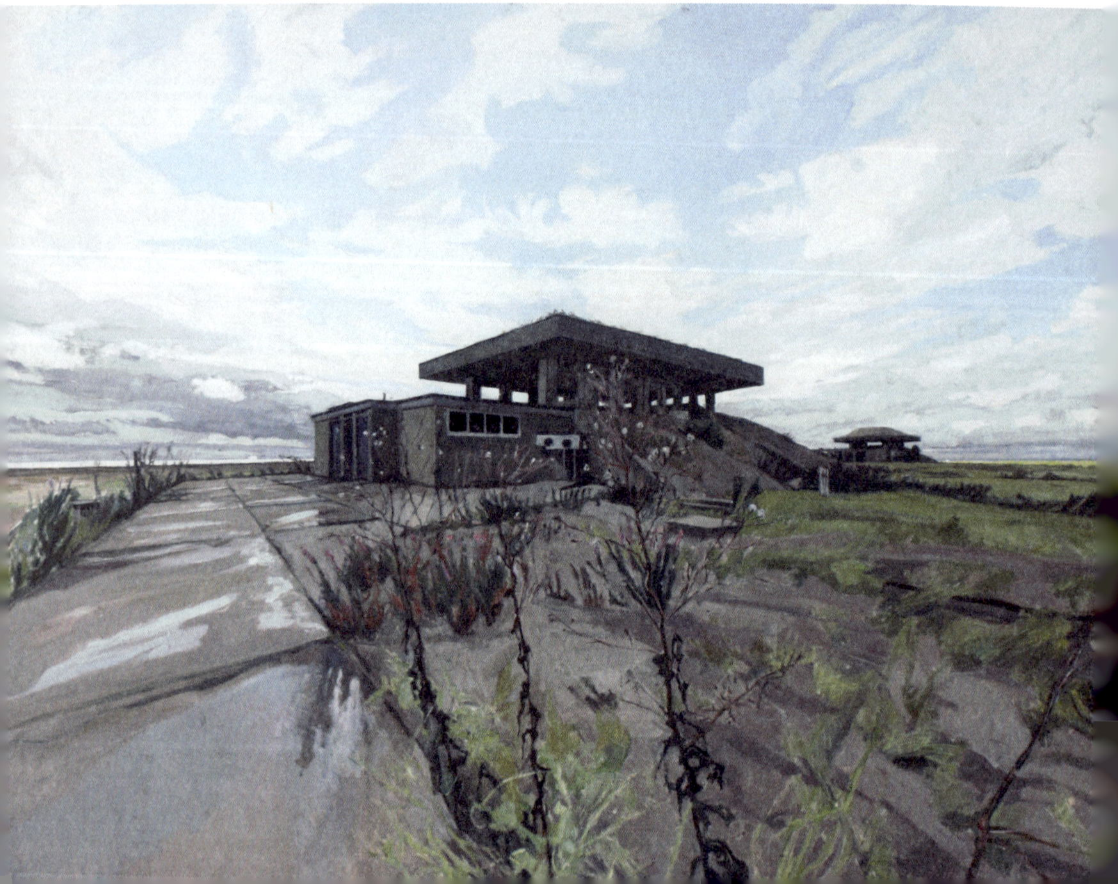

38. *Shingle Laboratory No.2 with Orford Church and Castle*, 1994–6
39. *Laboratory Pagodas Nos 4 & 5, Late Summer, Orford Ness*, 1992–5

40. *Estuary Mudflats: The Battle*, 1994–8

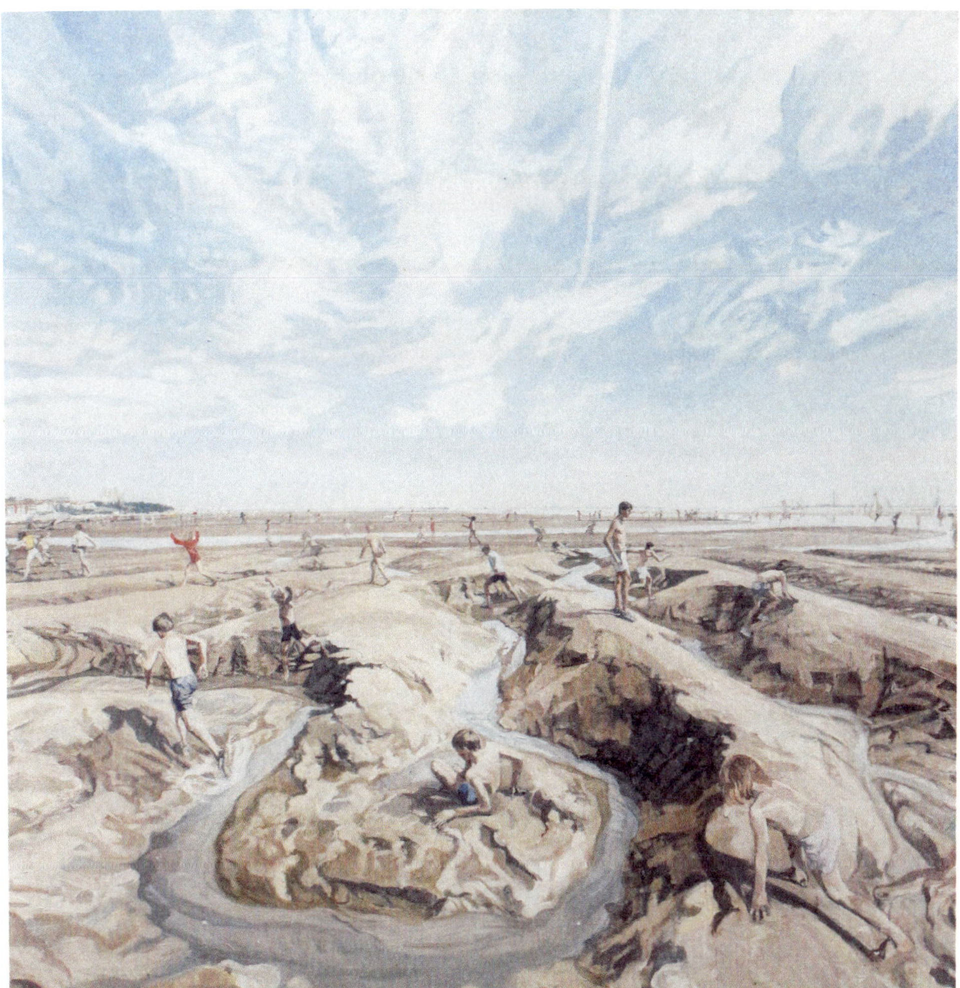

introduction by William Feaver, who was then, and has remained, an admirer of Wonnacott's paintings:

> The paintings have changed over the years (Wonnacott is an insatiable retoucher) and while the frolics have remained the same, the folds and runnels have been subject to reshaping. This is the landscape painter as God, looking down, seeing that the mud wasn't good enough, altering – as painters do, using their coloured mud and modifying with one end in mind, landscape truth as distinct from topographic accuracy.[61]

During the same period of the early 1990s, Wonnacott accepted a commission from the National Maritime Museum to paint the docks at Felixstowe, a port town on the Suffolk coast not far south of Orford. The museum wanted to record 'modern methods of cargo handling in order to help explain the continuing importance of sea-trade to Britain, despite the fact that ships are now largely unseen by the general population'.[62] He painted *Winter Afternoon,*

41. *Winter Afternoon, Container Ships off Felixstowe*, 1993–4

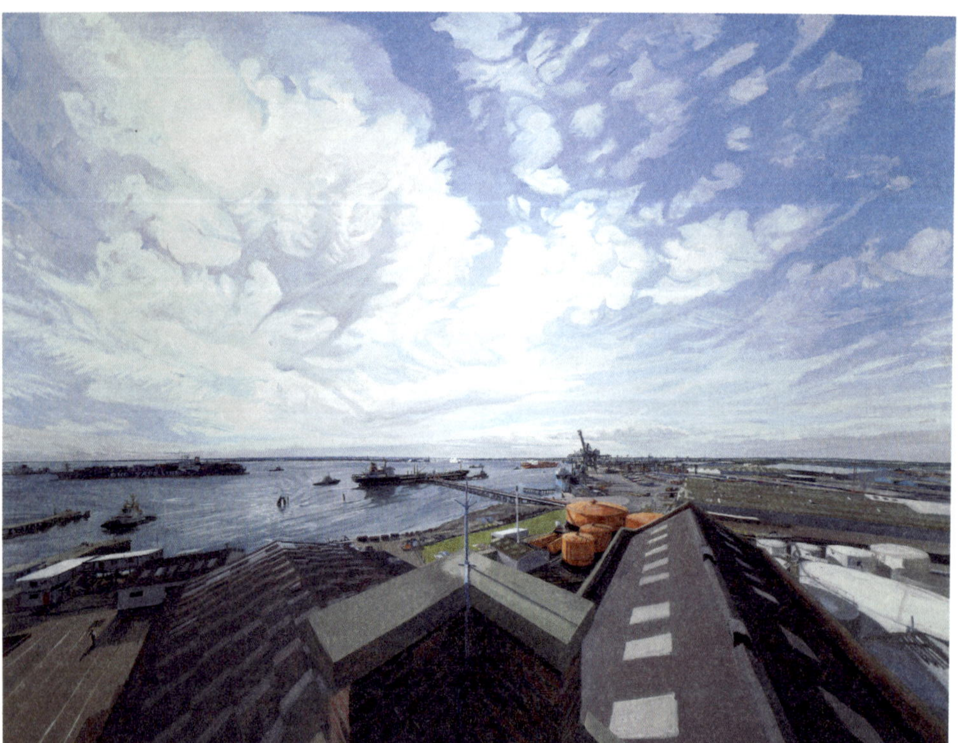

Container Ships off Felixstowe, a big, sunny view of the docks (fig.41). It was apparently a great disappointment to the Port of Lowestoft, which had been involved in the commission, because it was so studiously unheroic, documenting the appearance of the port, without any effort to glamorise it. Wonnacott remembers 'arranging my easels permanently on top of an old flour mill in the Felixstowe docks and eventually being marched off-site by the dock police after an angry dock manager failed to persuade me to concentrate my sights only on the modern dock construction'.[63] As he wrote:

> I paint as I live dominated by the anarchic splendours of the East Anglian sky. Sky provides the wild card in my painting. It floods each landscape with particular atmospheric light while fighting the elaborate formal plotting of my geometry.[64]

In his exhibition at Agnew's in 1996, Wonnacott exhibited more of his paintings of the seashore and marshland, close to his house in Chalkwell. There is *Estuary, Shelter with Young Girl Skating*, which shows a girl on roller skates going along the promontory underneath one of the council's seaside pavilions and *Estuary Crowstone: The Overflow with Girl about to Cartwheel* (fig.42). There is *Estuary, the Paddling Pool with Zofja Throwing Stones* (fig.43), a wide open expanse, singularly bleak, with almost no visual incident except a couple of pool spar markers, two windswept trees on the shoreline and Kent somewhere in the distance on the horizon.

There is a restrained poetry in these half-townscapes, half-seascapes, an anti-picturesque feeling of strong attachment to an urban setting which is as found, not composed for the artist or camera, inhabited by children without names, who are going about their lives on roller skates or turning cartwheels, studiously oblivious to the gaze of the artist, who views them only as incidents in a pictorial composition. Wonnacott is not the only artist in the post-war period to have been attracted to the anti-picturesque, the idea of Essex as a set of landscapes which represent a different side of England from the traditional rural idyll which has been celebrated perhaps too much over the last two centuries. Ken Worpole, a social historian, who was brought up in nearby Hadleigh and went to Southend Grammar School, has documented the appeal of this landscape in his book *350 Miles*, which describes

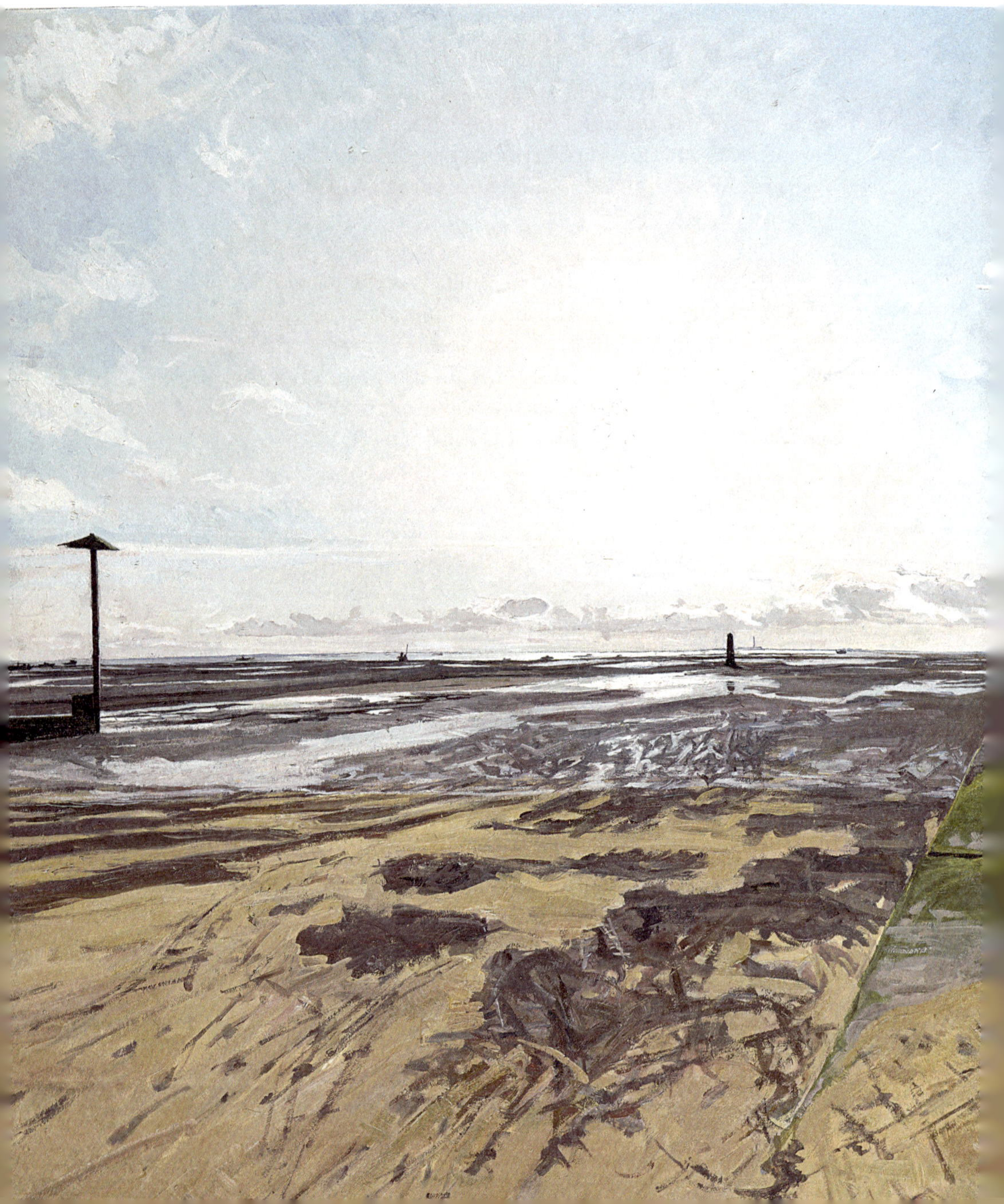

42. *Estuary Crowstone: The Overflow with Girl about to Cartwheel*, 1998

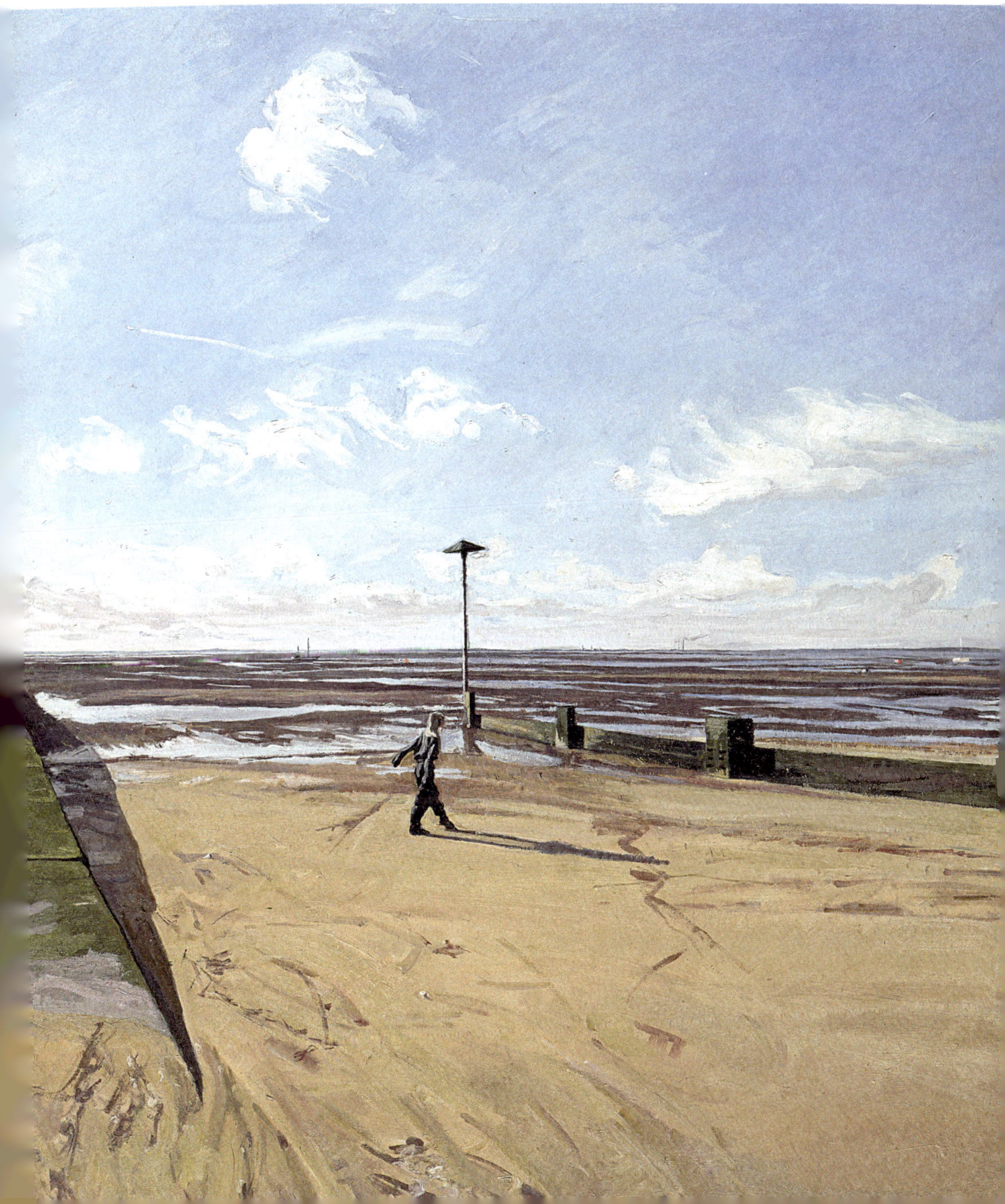

how other writers have been influenced by this part of the world, including Simon Schama, who begins his great book *Landscape and Memory* with his memories of visiting Leigh-on-Sea as a child, by 'the low, gull-swept estuary, the marriage bed of salt and fresh water, stretching as far as I could see from my northern Essex bank, toward a thin black horizon on the other side'.[65] In *The New English Landscape*, co-written with Jason Orton, Worpole has described how 'British topographical writing has been dominated in recent times by the landscapes of East Anglia, with an increasing interest in the particularities of estuarine Essex,' describing how the zeitgeist now favours 'a lonelier, bleaker, more rebarbative sense of place'.[66]

43. *Estuary, the Paddling Pool with Zofja Throwing Stones*, 1995–6

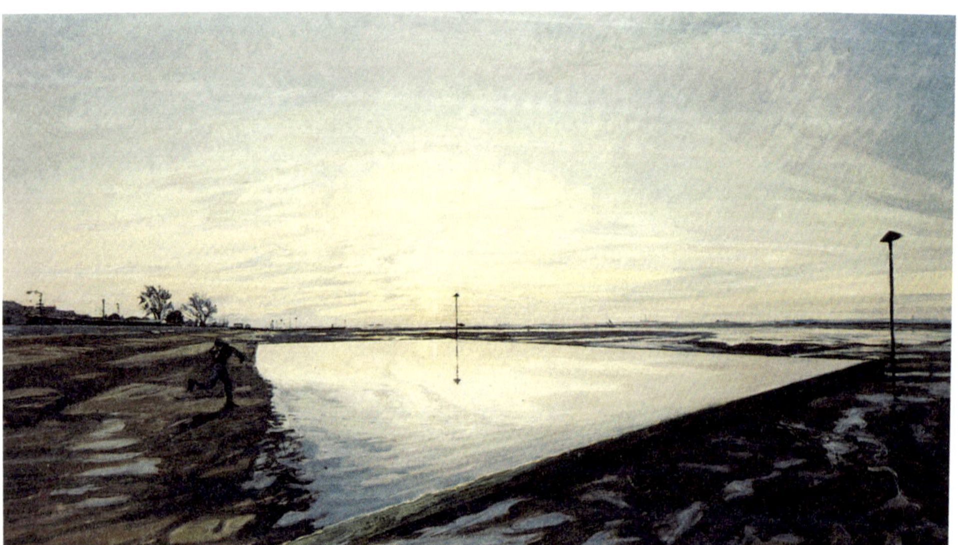

Chapter 9

The Royal Family

Wonnacott's painting of the Royal Family came about at the suggestion of Admiral Lord Lewin, the former Admiral of the Fleet, whom Wonnacott was painting for the National Maritime Museum as its departing Chairman (he occupied that role from 1987 to 1995). Lewin was depicted in the great Painted Hall at Greenwich, – where Nelson's body lay in state in January 1806 – standing in the uniform of the Admiral of the Fleet (fig.44). This was the type of commission that Wonnacott thrives on, making friends with the sitter, involving himself in the life of the institution, living in the officers' mess and celebrating the person and his role in a way that is not unctuous. Wonnacott tells how he was encouraged, half dared, to come to me as Director of the National Portrait Gallery:

> I was living in the officers' mess in Greenwich while I painted Lord Lewin and the Royal Naval College grounds. Terry Lewin and I were having a beer together after he had been standing for his portrait in the Painted Hall when we fell to discussing the Richard Rogers dome which was nearing completion across the river. We both thought it a poor celebration of the idea of entering a new millennium. Somehow we came to talk about the Queen Mother, remembering that she completed her centenary in this millennium year. I think that in the end I was almost dared to come and suggest a grand portrait of the core members of the Royal Family in the Palace. I doubt if either of us thought you'd buy the proposition any more than you thought the Palace might go along with us – too many risks.[67]

So, in the summer of 1998, John Wonnacott came to see me with what he thought was a bright idea. Since the Queen Mother was going to celebrate her hundredth birthday on 4 August 2000, he asked, 'Had the Gallery considered commissioning a portrait of the current royal lineage which could be shown as a family of four generations?'[68] The truth was, we hadn't. We were in the middle of a big building project, which we were hoping to open in 2000 as a way of celebrating the millennium. The traditional role of the National Portrait Gallery in acquiring portraits of members of the Royal Family was in abeyance. The last thing we wanted was a large, multi-generational royal portrait, not so long after the

44. *Admiral of the Fleet, Lord Lewin of Greenwich, in the Painted Hall*, 1995–8

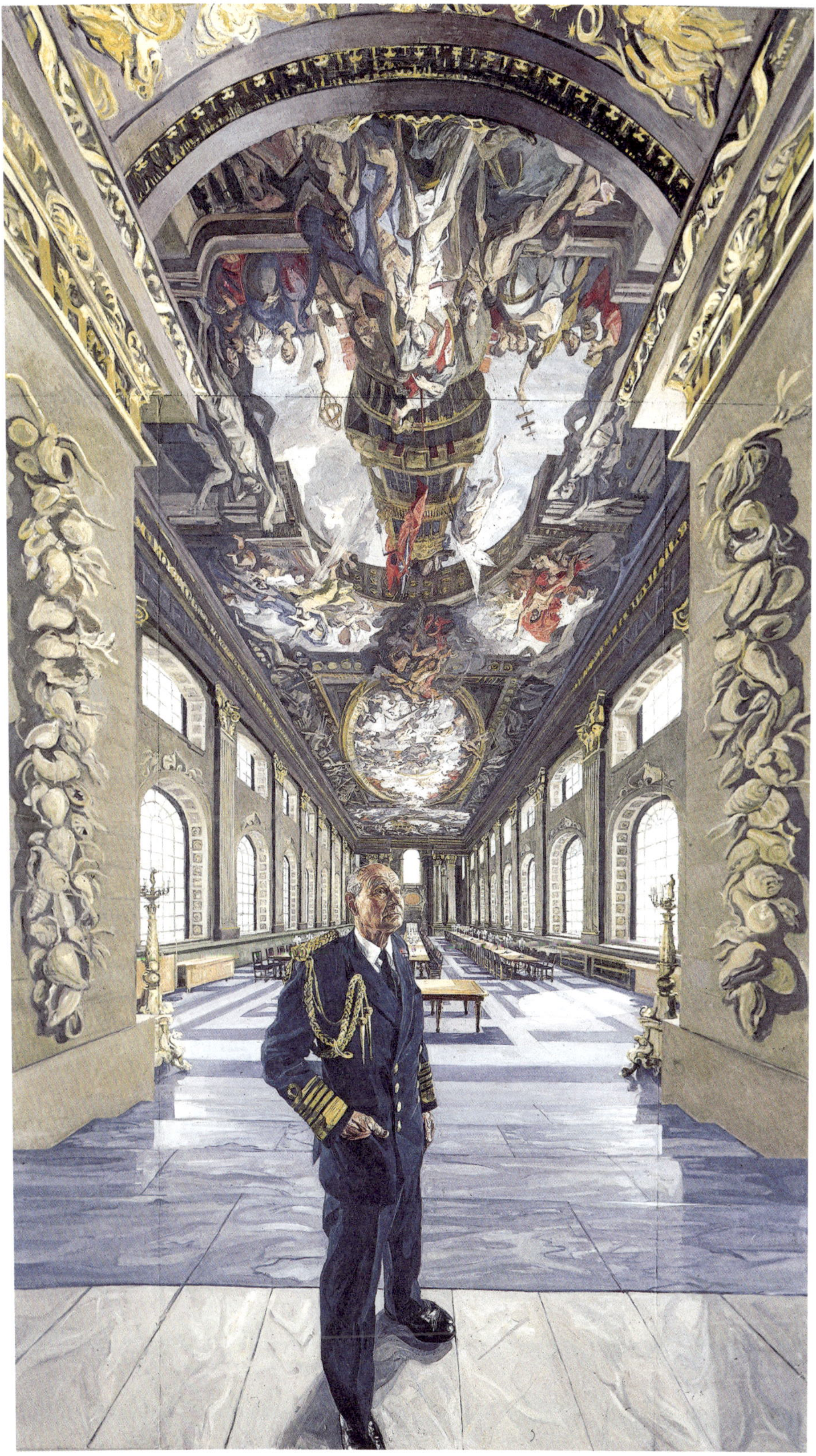

so-called *annus horribilis*, when so many fractures had appeared in the life of the Royal Family – Prince Andrew had separated from his wife, Sarah Ferguson; Princess Anne had got divorced; it had become known that Prince Charles was having an affair with Camilla Parker Bowles; and Windsor Castle had had a big fire.

I told Wonnacott that I would write to Buckingham Palace to ask if it was possible, confident that they would say no. On 31 July 1998, just before going away on holiday, I wrote to Robert Fellowes, the Queen's private secretary:

> I wanted to consult you about an idea which has been suggested to us by the artist, John Wonnacott, who, as you may have seen, recently completed a large and very successful portrait of John Major for us.
>
> Following on from his portraits of John Major and another fine, large-scale portrait of Admiral Lewin for the National Maritime Museum, he has asked whether or not the Trustees of the National Portrait Gallery might consider commissioning a group portrait of the Royal Family to mark the millennium.
>
> Initially I have to admit I was slightly sceptical of the idea. We already have the portrait of Her Majesty by Pietro Annigoni, which still looks well; the Bryan Organ painting of the Prince of Wales, which we are loaning to Bodelwyddan Castle in North Wales for a period of two months to help them; and the controversial portrait of the Queen Mother by Alison Watt. But John Wonnacott then pointed out that there has not been a family portrait since Sir James Gunn's 'Conversation Piece at the Royal Lodge, Windsor' in 1950; and that now is a rather unique moment in the history of the Royal Family when it might be possible to depict four generations together (i.e. the Queen Mother, the Queen, Prince Philip, Prince Charles and Princes William and Harry). Also, I cannot think of any other artist who would be able to undertake such an ambitious commission and execute it in such a way that it would fit appropriately within the existing tradition of twentieth-century royal portraiture.

I realise that you may feel that this is not worth taking further, since royal portraits are so frequently controversial; but I feel that there would be a special appropriateness to such a commission if it were to be unveiled in the year 2000 at the time that our new wing is opened.[69]

They said yes.

What followed was a year of sittings with the individual members of the Royal Family. One of Wonnacott's special talents is that he is somehow able to inveigle himself into any situation, while remaining entirely unchanged in his attitude, which was probably a good way for him to deal with the Royal Family, who I suspect preferred his admirable straightforwardness to the obsequiousness they must so often have to endure. He studied them to show the truth of their individual personalities, not too deferentially, both as members of a modern family, with all the tensions and dysfunctions that involves, and as the Royal Family, with the ceremony and deference that requires.

Royal portraiture is an incredibly difficult genre to get right. The White Drawing Room, which is the setting for the portrait, is a room of almost absurd over-grandiosity, with too many chandeliers, and so much ornamental gilding that draws the viewer's attention away from the central drama of the relationship between the six sitters, representing four different generations. Each of the sitters was drawn in turn, separately from the others – the Queen Mother in Clarence House in April 1999, William and Harry at Eton. Wonnacott enjoyed doing it, even if it was daunting:

All I had to do every single time was to psyche myself up so that I didn't just get side-tracked into finding the occasion interesting, and instead looked and drew like crazy so as to get the maximum information out of each session.[70]

He asked them to pose in the way he wanted, which was not always straightforward. He describes what it was like to paint the Queen Mother:

Painting the Queen Mother in Clarence House was an extraordinary experience. I would turn up two

45. *Head of Prince William II*, 1999–2000

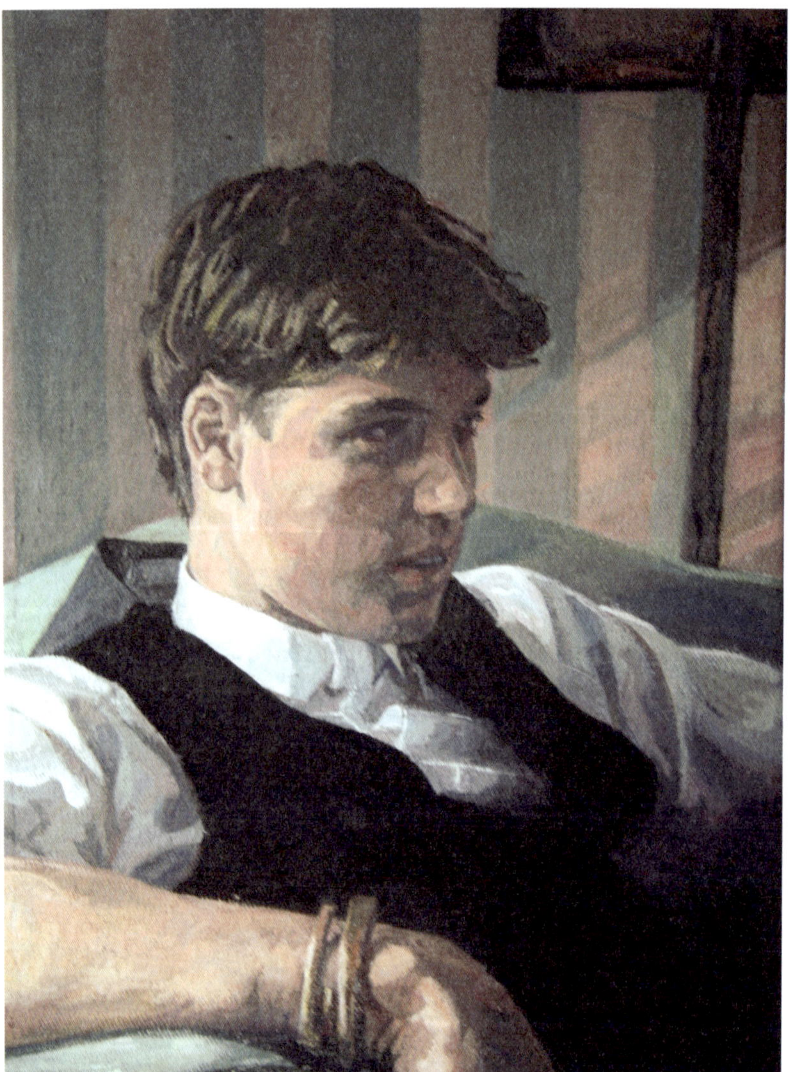

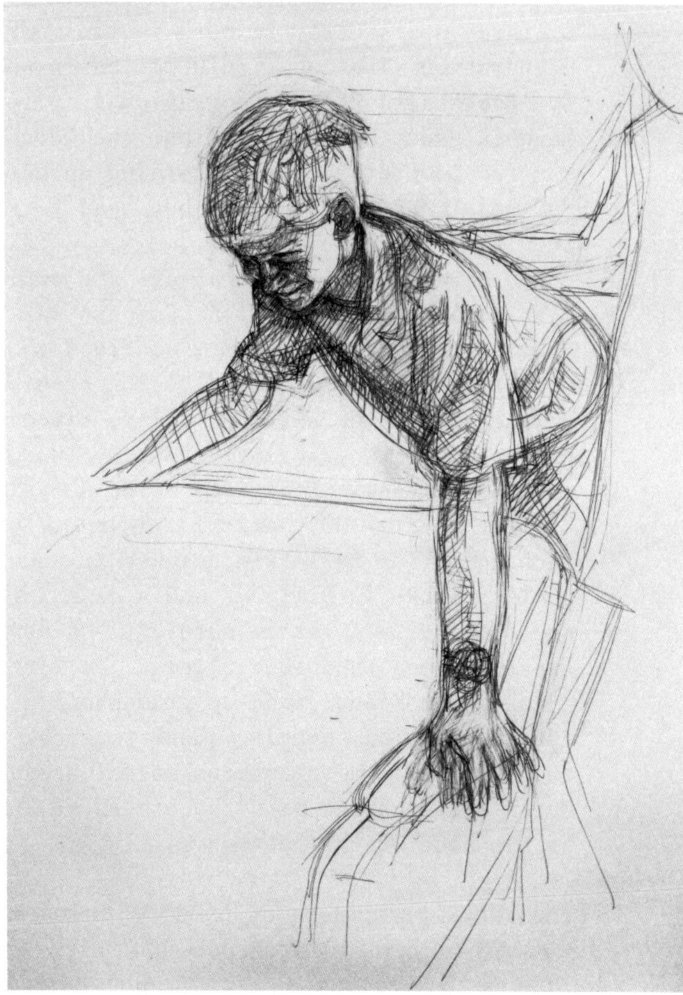

46. *Study for Prince Harry*, 1999–2000

or three hours early to work in the room in preparation. Then she would be led in an hour later by 'Backstairs Billy' to graciously offer me her hand in greeting. When posing, the Queen Mother was the complete actress, holding up her hand just so when I asked or turning her head to smile as required. Often in a break, we would take a walk round her collection and always she would tell me with relish of how her fine Cézanne was bought for just 60 pounds. Her equerry confided to me in a whisper that 60 pounds had been the shipping cost. At the end of the sitting, always timed for lunch, HM would depart graciously towards the chatter and clink of glasses of a party a few doors away – not bad for nearly 100 years old. Then Billy would come back and offer 'a little drinkee Mr Wonnacott?' – 'Yes thank you Billy' – and a glass of Chablis would appear. 'A little sarnie?' – a neatly squared smoked salmon sandwich followed. 'A little music?' – an old fashioned wind-up gramophone played Fred Astaire singing 'dancing cheek to cheek' – it was quite unreal. The painted sketch I produced of the Queen Mother hangs with the others at Highgrove and is the best of the lot.[71]

The sketches, particularly of Prince William and Prince Harry, give a sense of their respective personalities (figs 45, 46). Wonnacott painted a large number of oil sketches based on the drawings and hundreds of photographs to try to convey a sense of their individual characters, as well as drawings to work out the overall composition. Painting the Queen was trickier.

The Queen is not an actress like her mother. She doesn't trouble to pose artfully or even to sit still but talks continuously – about her trips (she doesn't at all share my love for coastal mud for example) and about her children with warm humour. While she didn't, I think, enjoy acting out roles in the painting, for the last quarter of an hour of each sitting, she always cooperated fully and even made suggestions. I had just one session, with only her out of the family, in the White Drawing Room, with

47. *The Royal Family: A Centenary Portrait*, 2000

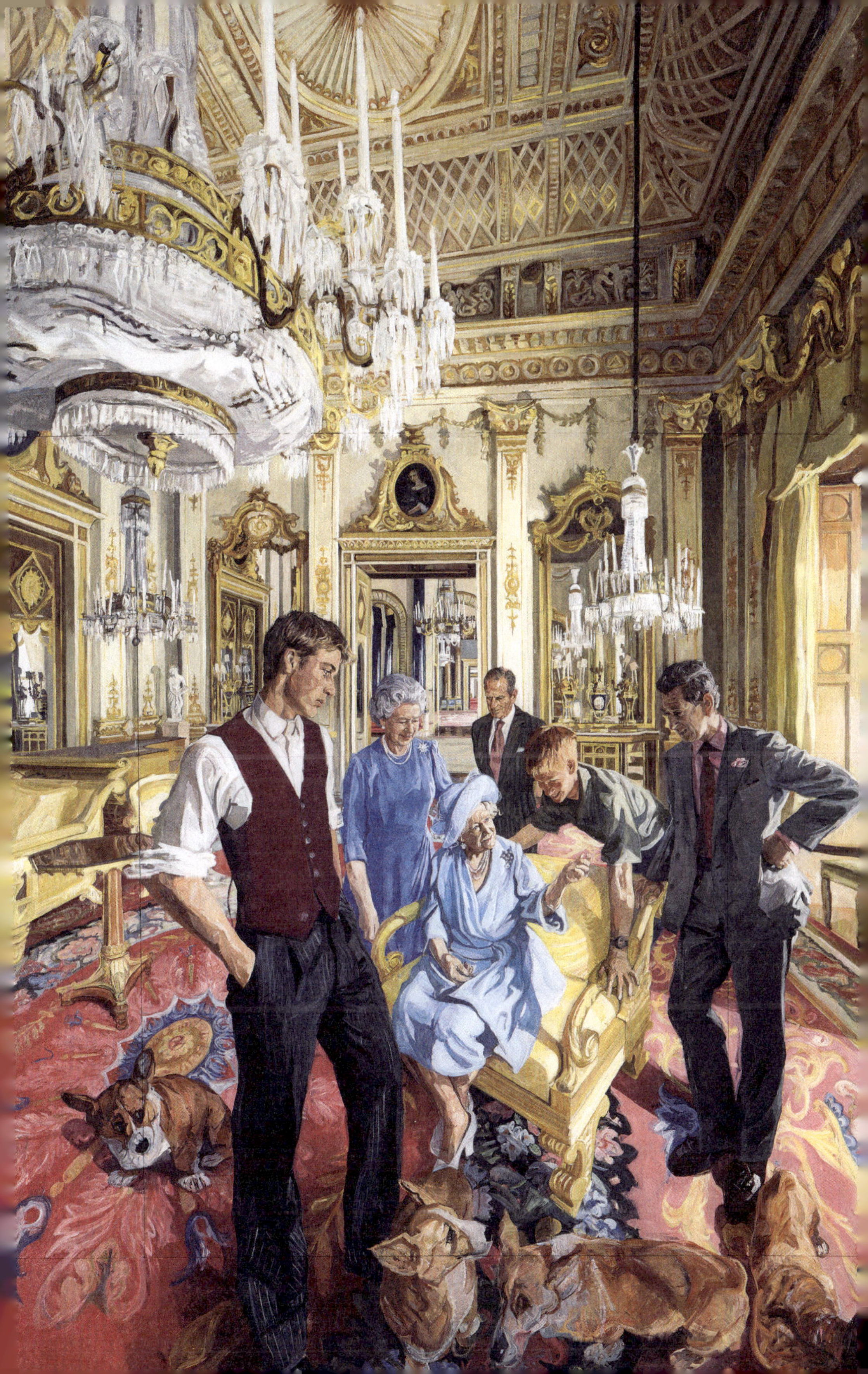

all the furniture in place. Without the opportunity to get Her Majesty to pose leaning over the golden couch to where her mother would be sitting in my painting, I could never have completed the arrangement and scale of the figures.[72]

The result is, of necessity, a very carefully constructed image of modern monarchy, highly self-conscious in the way it depicts the relationships between members of the family, with Prince Harry leaning over the arm of the yellow chair to talk to the Queen Mother, the Prince of Wales more casually beside them, Prince William very tall and to one side, and with the Queen and the Duke of Edinburgh in the centre of the composition (fig.47).

In the choice of room in which to paint the Royal Family and its overall composition, the painting was deliberately based on Sir John Lavery's *The Royal Family at Buckingham Palace* (1913; NPG 1745). If anyone has the capacity to add a new dimension to the genre of royal portraiture, it is Wonnacott. This work commemorates a particular moment in the Royal Family's life, with four generations surrounding the Queen Mother not long before she died: it is a monument to monarchy and what it had meant during the 20th century. But we no longer live in an age of deference. We now know them too well from television and photography and the casual invasiveness of speculative newspaper journalism.

The picture is magnificent, a composition of great and heroically complex invention, reinvigorating the tradition of royal portraiture, but it is no longer on public display. On the other hand, the sketches which were made for it still hang at Highgrove, the Prince of Wales's private house in Gloucestershire, as a memento of his grandmother and members of his close family at the end of her life.

Chapter 10

Self-Portraits and Friends

Wonnacott held an exhibition at Agnew's in September 2005. It included an unusual number of self-portraits. The artist was in his mid-sixties, in reflective mood. The moment when he might have expected to be esteemed for a long and successful career found him instead in an environment in which figurative painting had moved right outside the mainstream into a backwater occupied only by the Royal Society of Portrait Painters, which elected him an Honorary Member in 2001.

Wonnacott is a remarkable painter of himself, normally in the first-floor room where he paints, sometimes shown as a painting within a painting, with the different moods of the seasons and the weather in the background, the mudflats of the estuary and the evening sky. In the early 1990s, he depicted himself in a black jersey at night (fig.48) and painted studies of himself in connection with the two portraits acquired by the Tate and the Metropolitan Museum (fig.49). Ten years later, painting himself had become a routine, if not an obsession, including *Self-Portrait: Winter Sunset* (fig.50) and with palette in hand and an open-necked red shirt (p.6). They are not exactly exercises in self-analysis, more in the art and practice of painting, demonstrations of the way that painting can reveal so much more about a person than a photograph. There are few people who are able to paint themselves so vividly, clinically and dispassionately.

Wonnacott also paints his friends, two in particular. Ian Cox, a local painter, sat for him in the early 1990s (fig.54). His other close friend, Professor Bernard de Neumann (or Bernhard von Neumann, the name by which he is known in Germany and Austria), was a mathematician who worked for Marconi and the Ministry of Defence, before becoming Professor of Mathematics at City University, London, in 1988. He appears in an early portrait with a large beer glass in hand (fig.51). Cox and Neumann appear in the background of Wonnacott's *Studio Conversation 1*, owned by Tate Britain (see fig.33). In the second half of the 1990s, he used them as convenient models for Rabelaisian pictures of feasting, oysters on the table and much wine, studies of friendship and conviviality (fig.52). Between 2001 and 2005, he painted a picture of Neumann slumped in a chair in the studio, older and more reflective and probably more melancholy (fig.55). Wonnacott showed it in the annual exhibition of the Royal Society of Portrait Painters. It won the annual Ondaatje Prize for Portraiture.

48. *Night Portrait, Black Jersey*, 1989–92

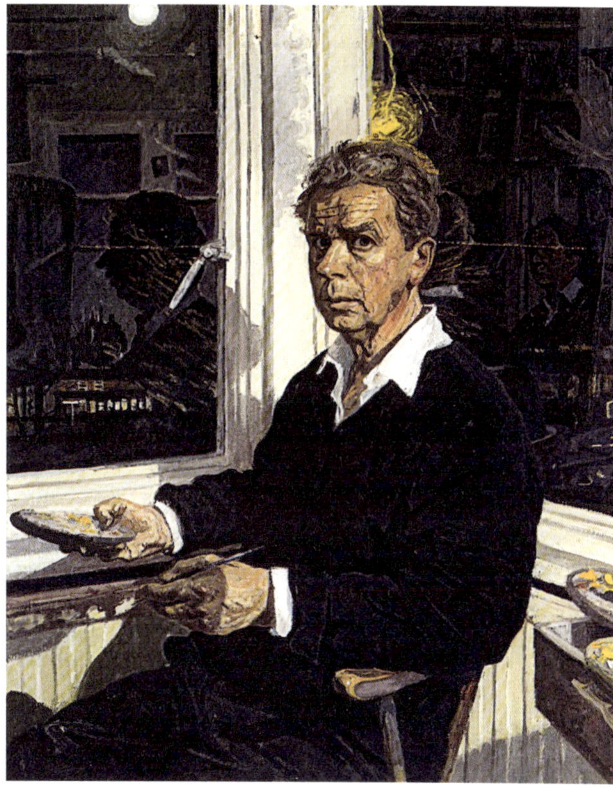

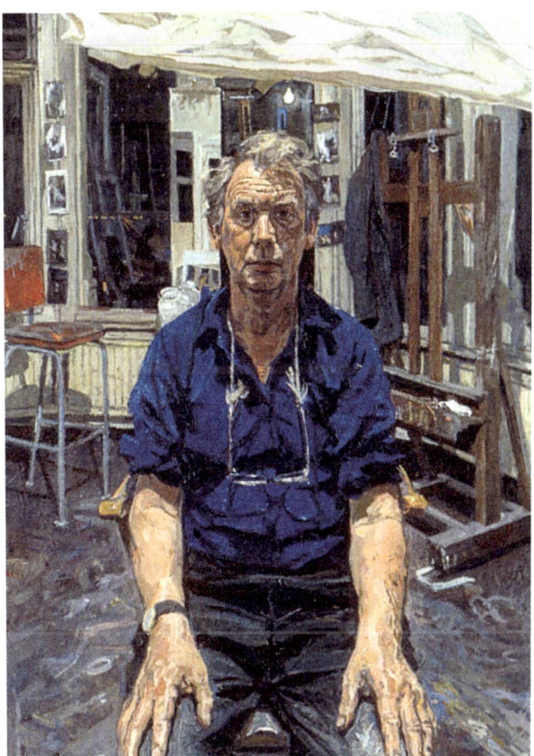

49. *Small Portrait, Met Study*, 1992–5

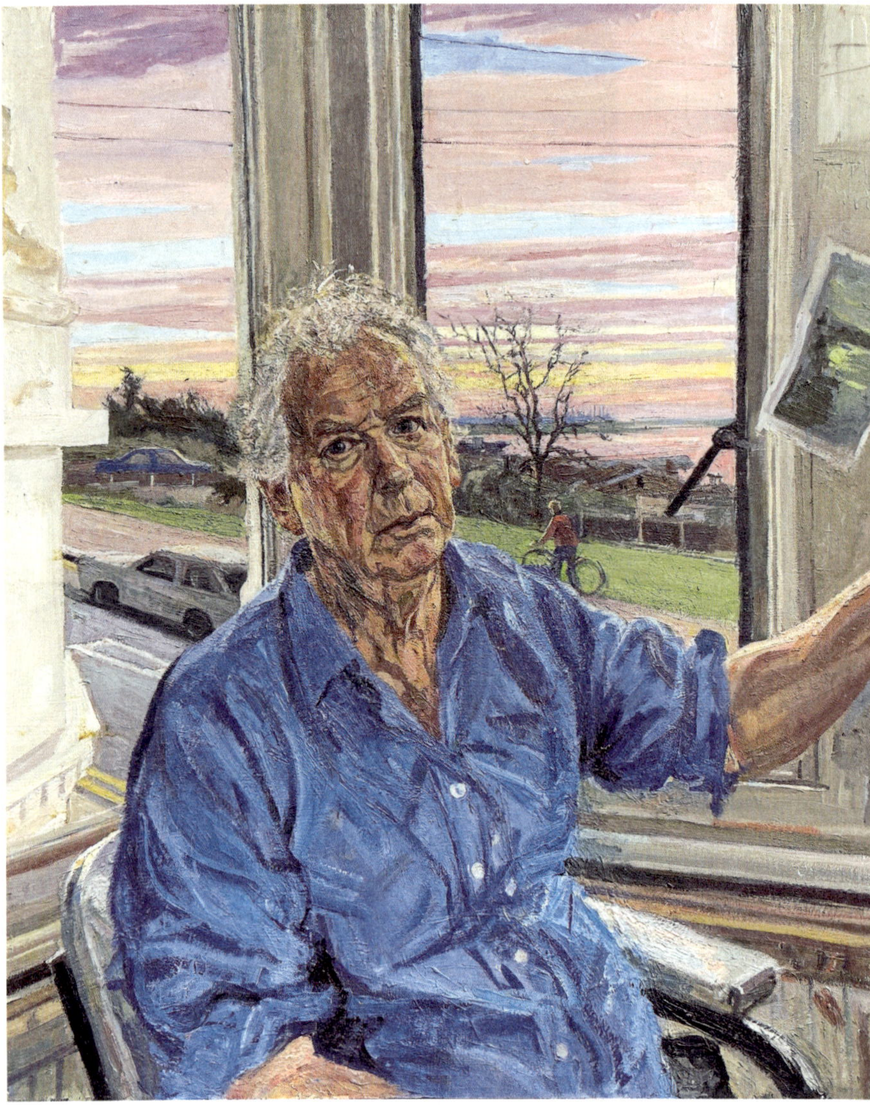

50. *Self-Portrait, Winter Sunset*, 2004–5

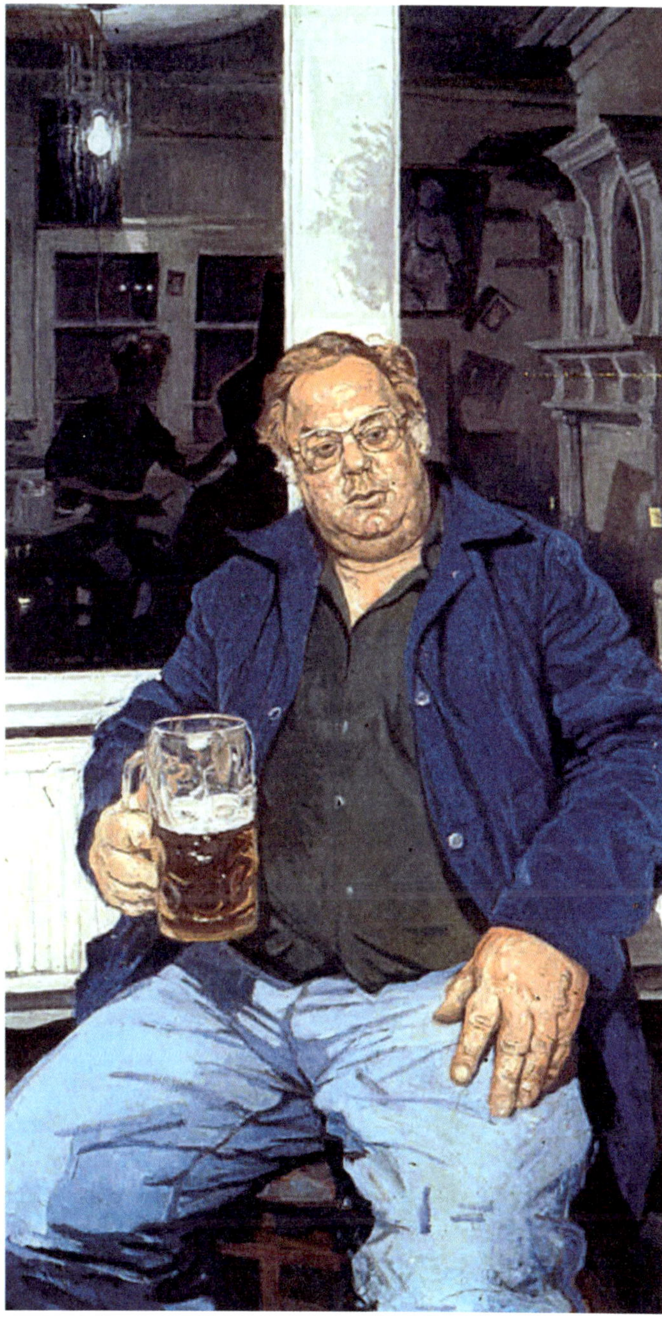

51. *The Mathematician I*, 1990–1

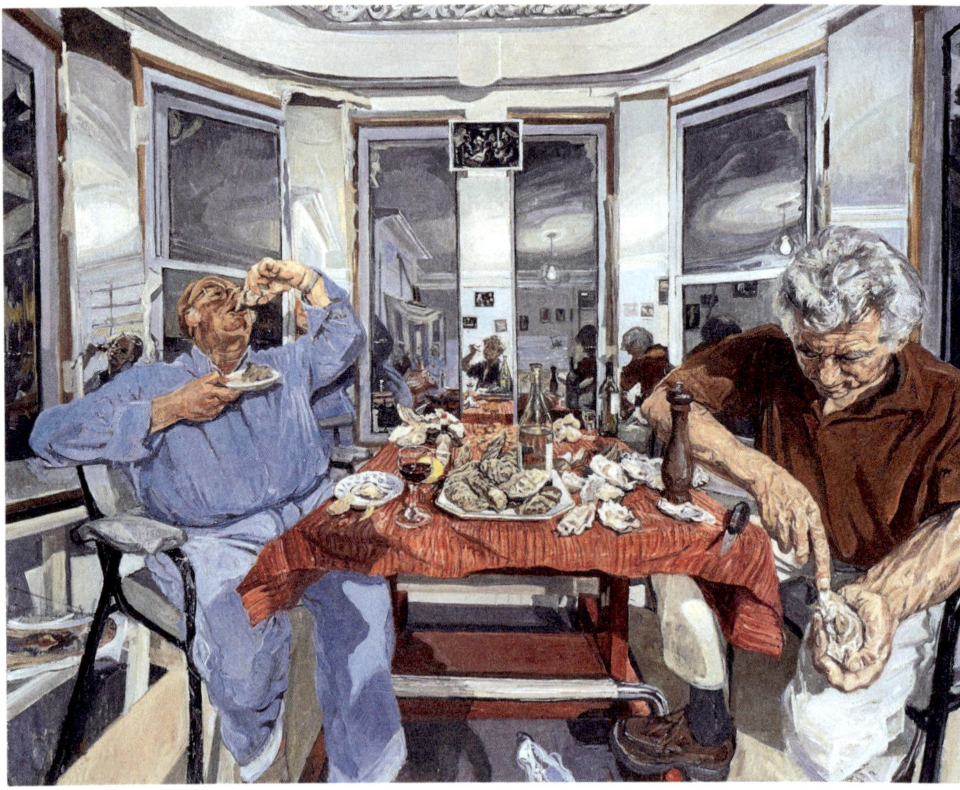

52. *Red Tablecloth II, Oyster Eaters*, 1996–9

Not included in his exhibition at Agnew's, though it probably should have been, was Wonnacott's portrait of Edwin ('Jim') Manton, the great Constable collector, who had lived in Westcliff-on-Sea as a child before migrating first to Paris and then New York, where he was one of the key figures in the development of AIG, a big international insurance firm, its President from 1942 to 1969 and then its Chairman.[73] Manton was a great admirer of Wonnacott's paintings, collected them, and invited Wonnacott to come and see him in his office when he was in New York for his exhibition at Hirschl and Adler in 1999.

> It resulted from drawings I made when relaxing with him over a cup of tea in his suite of offices where he presided in emeritus splendour as ex-chairman of AIG. Jim had asked me to call in on him when I was in New York for my Hirschl and Adler show in 1999. He already owned a large Wonnacott Leigh

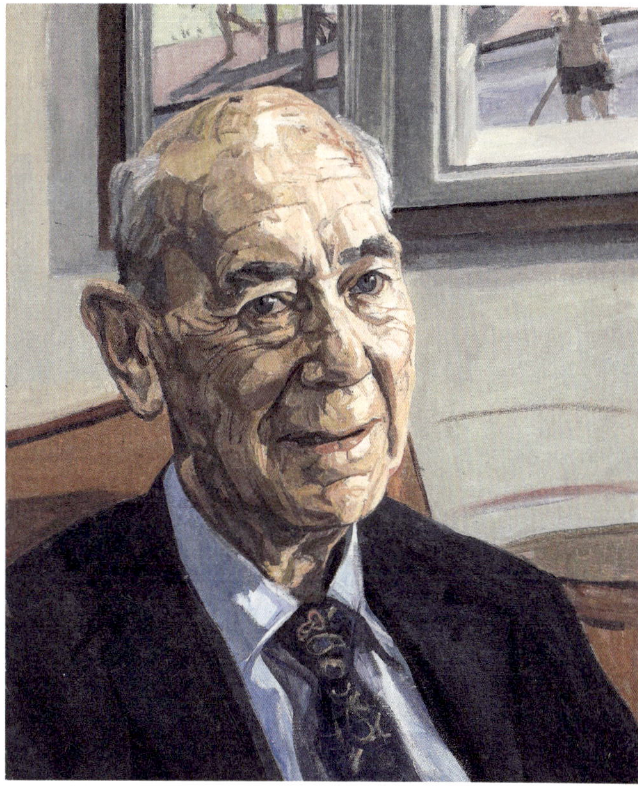

53. *Portrait of Jim Manton*, 2000

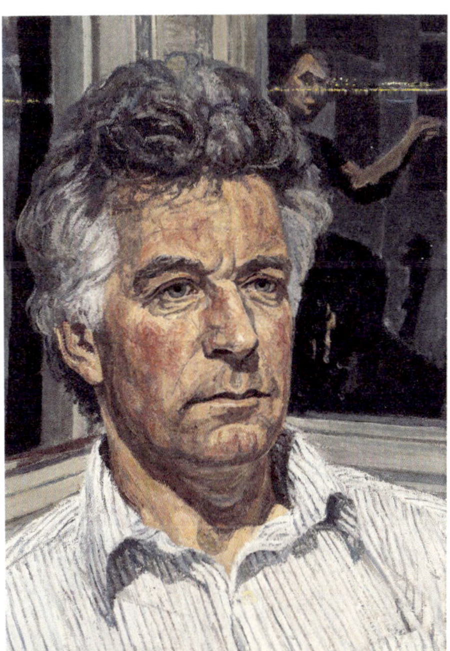

54. *Ian with Striped Shirt*, 1991–2

Window painting which hung behind his desk among the Constables and Turners – and it needed cleaning. I promised to get it cleaned for him if he commissioned me to paint from the 94th floor balconies looking down on Broadway, the fish market and across to the twin towers. When he agreed, I spat on the picture while he was out of the office, wiped off the coffee and demanded my contract. As a businessman, he was so impressed by my effrontery that he gave me the contract and I began drawing a few weeks later. He flew me to New York and put me up in an apartment on Water Street where I also made two rather splendid city drawings. It came as a shock to [Director of the Tate] Nick Serota when he was visiting Manton 'on the scrounge', when I emerged from the balcony into the office.[74]

The portrait which resulted from this encounter was subsequently bought by the Tate as a way of recognising the generosity of one its greatest benefactors (fig.53). It hangs to the left of the door of the so-called Manton Entrance to Tate Britain in the basement off Atterbury Street, seen by many, but not necessarily appreciated.

55. *The Mathematician, Professor Bernard de Neumann*, 2001–4

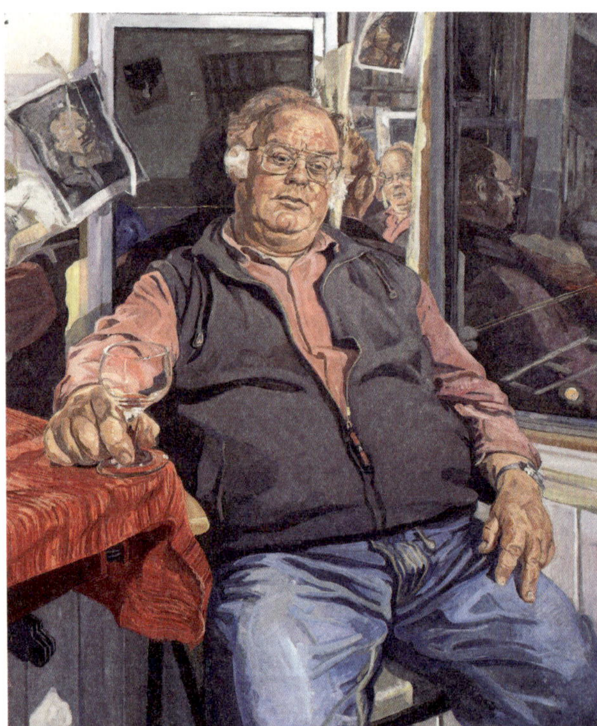

Chapter 11

Late Works

56. *Putting on Ballet Shoe 2, Young Dancers Prepare for Class while Seniors Practise Jumps*, 2008–10

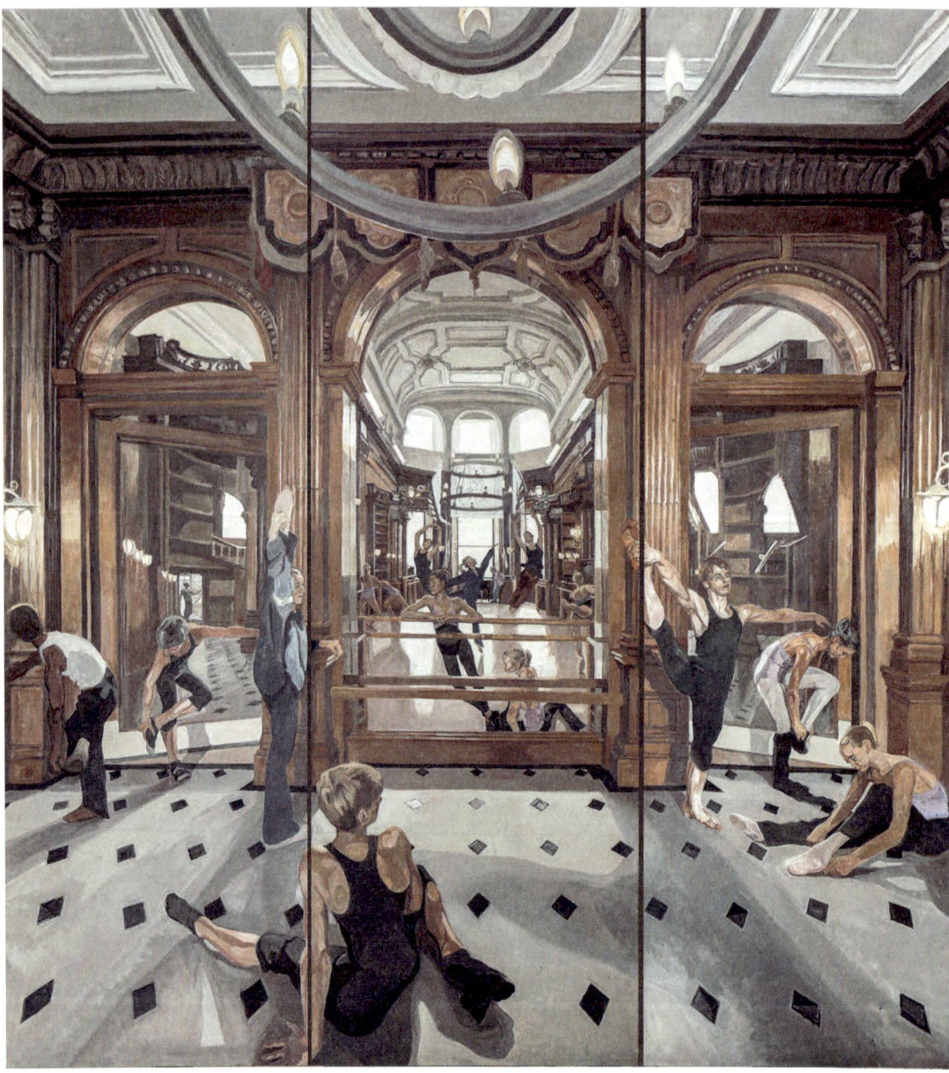

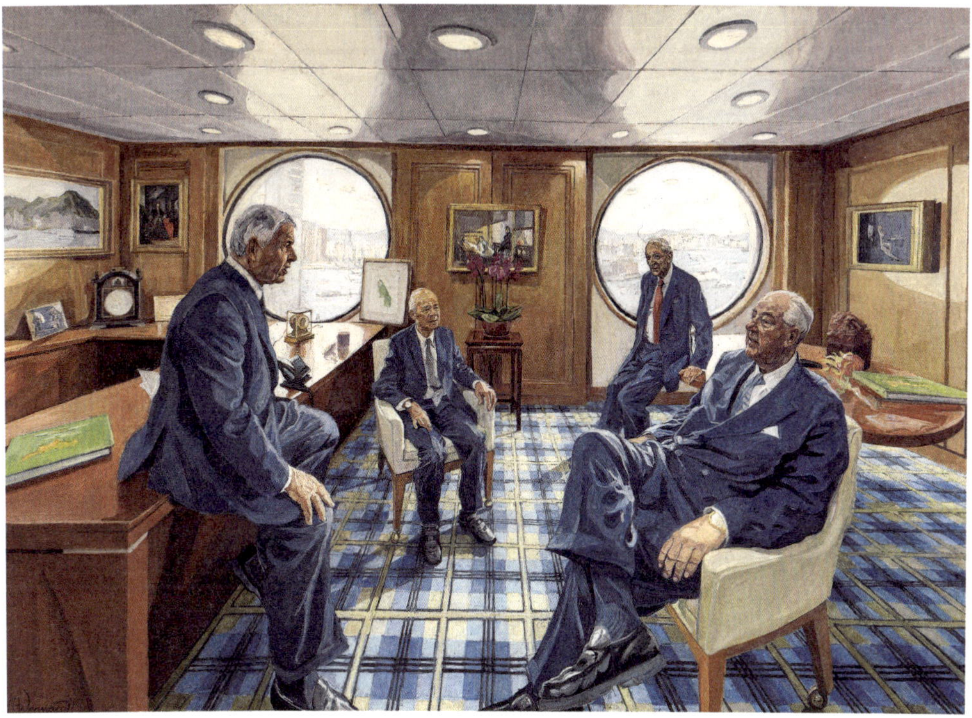

57. *Taipans on the 48th Floor*, 2012–13

Wonnacott's last exhibition at Agnew's was held in 2011, after the gallery had moved from its luxurious accommodation in Bond Street to a smaller space in Albemarle Street. It was, as Wonnacott himself described it, the first of his exhibitions 'to show no paintings of the estuary or my family and local friends'. Instead, he was preoccupied by issues connected with mortality – he had had a brush with death, following, as he describes it, 'a fifty-year diet of alcohol and cholesterol' – and his long-standing interest in the psychology of perception, 'in order to clarify, at least for myself, the instinctive decision, made during the 1960s, not to follow Picasso's 1907 rejection of single viewpoint looking, which has led many fine painters to explore exclusively flat invention over the past century'.[75]

In 2007, when his son Jack began training at Tring Park School for the Performing Arts, John arranged to draw and paint there two days a week, taking the opportunity offered to study spatial shape and movement created in performance in the richly decorated interiors of one of the group of Rothschild mansions in

58. *Self-Portrait with an Apple for G*, 2017

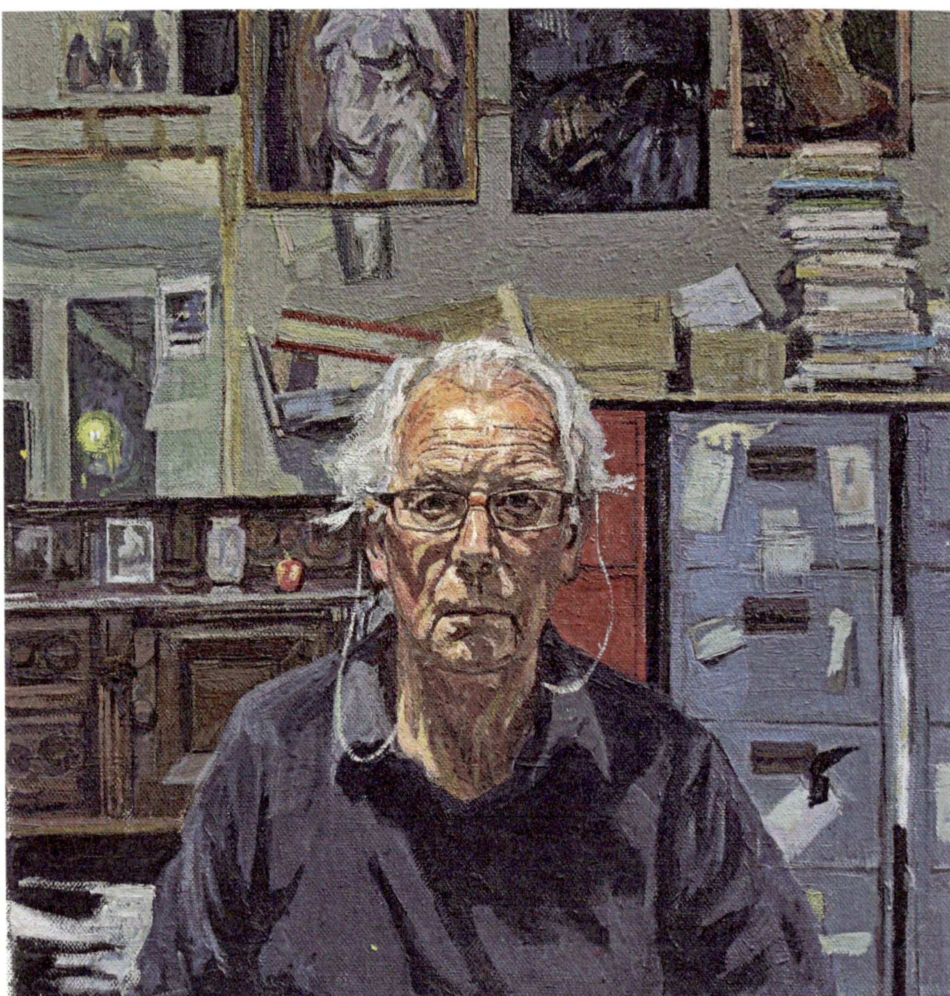

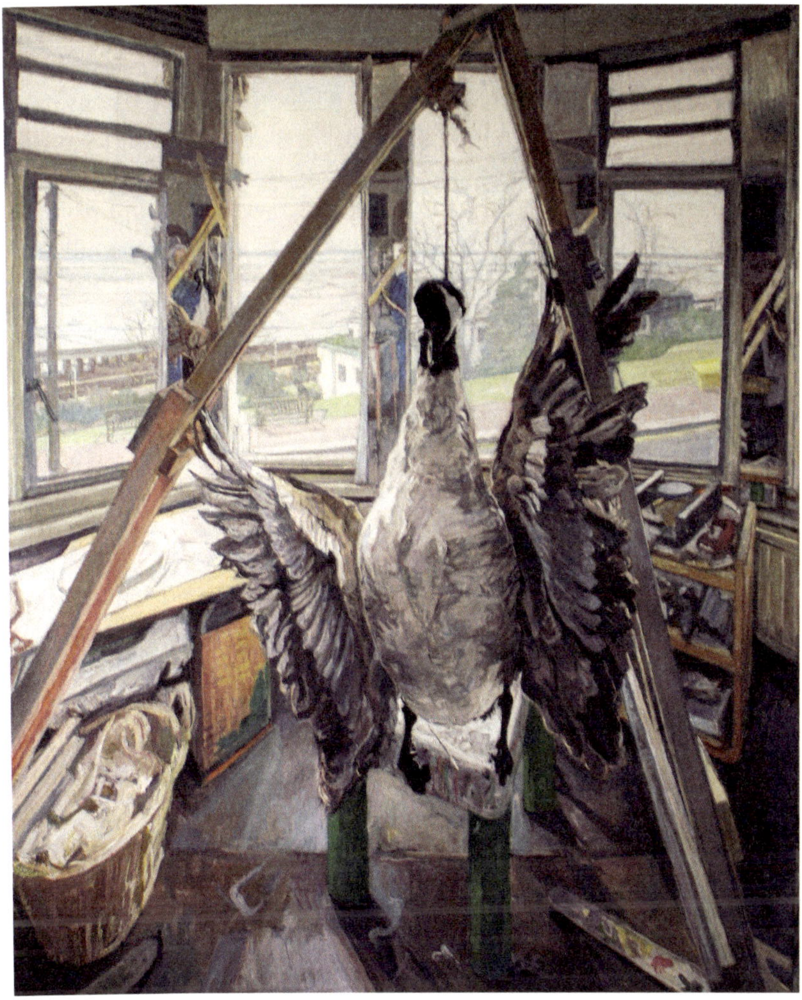

59. *Hanging Goose, Day*, 2017

Buckinghamshire. John would arrive before class with a van loaded with easels and sections of painting board to be bolted together on site. This group of four 8 × 4-foot paintings are the most self-consciously elaborate and performative works in his oeuvre, highly sophisticated as exercises in their use of perspective (fig.56). In the same exhibition, he showed work he had done at Manderston in Berwickshire, where he made a series of paintings based on the production of a film by Stephen Evans. He set up a studio in an unused cowshed and arranged his Perspex perspective frames strategically across the mansion and garden – running from site to site as the crew moved round the estate.

Since the 2011 exhibition, he has occupied himself mostly with familiar subjects – paintings of himself, his close family and of the Thames estuary, as seen from the coast. He was also approached in late 2011 to undertake a major commission to paint the two Keswick brothers, who had ruled over the great Scottish trading company Jardine Matheson, in Hong Kong, for more than half a century, and their partners, Rodney Leach and Robert Kwok. This is the classic type of nearly impossible commission; indeed, there are very few artists nowadays who would have the technical ability to undertake it. Painted in the boardroom on the 48th floor of Jardine House in Hong Kong, it conveys the personality of the four partners well – Henry Keswick, the Chairman, seated in the foreground, the dominant figure, close to retirement after nearly 60 years with the firm; Simon, his youngest brother, half sitting, with Robert Kwok and Rodney Leach, both long-standing partners, in the background (fig.57).

There is also a late self-portrait, which shows the artist older, less ebullient, more reflective, fixing the spectator with his stare (fig.58).

He has painted a picture which he calls *Hanging Goose, Day* (2017), based on a goose which he bought in Harrison's, the local butchers in Leigh-on-Sea, after it had been shot by accident on the mudflats (fig.59). As he describes it: 'This, in its immediacy and colour, is the most "in awe of Velázquez" painting I have ever made. Even the paint rag basket and trolley still life seem to me a tribute to the master magician.'[76]

He has painted Grenfell Tower in its horror, a monument to the casualness of the local council in allowing a block of flats to be covered in material which was known to be flammable, causing many of its inhabitants to die in a nocturnal blaze, leaving the carcass of the building as a gaunt monument to a public disaster (fig.60).

One of Wonnacott's most recent works is *Self-Portrait with Grünewald and Two Geese* (see fig.61), which shows him at the height of his powers – thoughtful, self-reflective, confident of his position within history, sitting below two images of works that have influenced him and which are on a shelf in his studio: a large reproduction of the Crucifixion from Grünewald's *Isenheim Altarpiece* (1512–15) and an early pencil sketch of a Rubens *Crucifixion* from the Wallace Collection (now regarded as a late 17th-century copy), drawn in his second year at the Slade. He is sitting in his upstairs studio in Chalkwell, flanked by two pictures of geese, which have been tests of his artistic powers, a challenge of artistic representation. The painting is a homage to Velázquez, the biggest single influence of his career, who likewise single-mindedly pursued issues of depiction and attitudes to portraiture.

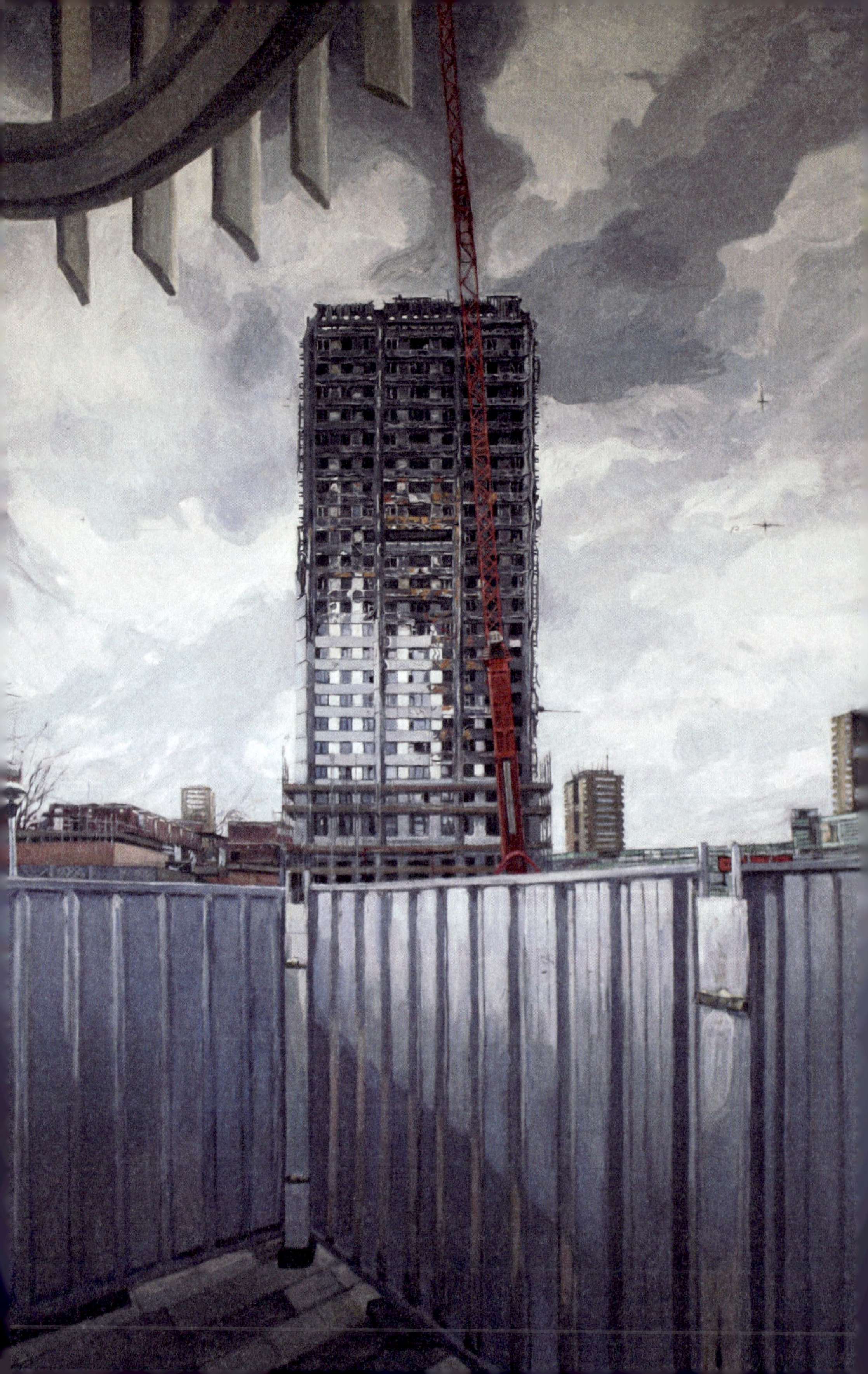

Chapter 12

Critical Reflections

Opposite
60. *Grenfell Tower, Winter*, 2017–18

In his introduction to Wonnacott's 1992 exhibition at Agnew's, the conservative critic Giles Auty began with a quotation from the late Sir Ernst Gombrich's introduction to the 12th edition of his bestselling *Story of Art*:

> When I first conceived and wrote the introduction and the chapter on experimental art I took it for granted that it was the duty of the critic and of the historian to explain and to justify all artistic experiments in the face of hostile criticism. Today the problem is rather that the shock has worn off and that almost anything experimental seems acceptable to the press and the public. If anybody needs a champion today it is the artist who shuns rebellious gestures.[77]

There is, of course, much truth in this comment. Until the Second World War, public taste in art, and that of the majority of critics, was highly conservative. Majority opinion, apart from a relatively small number of modernist critics, was in favour of a view of art which felt that it could, and should, be taught; that it involved an element of skill in practice which was the subject of informed critical judgement; and that the practice of art should be influenced by a good knowledge of the traditions of Old Master painting.

In 2017, the National Galleries of Scotland held a deliberately revisionist exhibition, *True to Life: British Realist Painting in the 1920s and 1930s*, demonstrating the quality and interest of realist painting of the period between the two world wars and its affinities to American painting of the same period, including the work of Edward Hopper and Thomas Hart Benton.[78] It made clear the extent to which the history of British painting in the early 20th century has been written in terms of a straightforward trajectory towards abstraction, the heroes being those who embraced modernity, whose work was supported by the critics and intellectuals of the time – Henry Moore, Paul Nash, Ben Nicholson – while the losers in the way that history has been written, but not their popularity at the time, were those who clung to old traditions. But in each generation there are artists, like Stanley Spencer and L.S. Lowry in the 1930s, who choose not to ally themselves with the avant-garde and to paint in their own way, with their highly individual and particular view of the world. In every generation, there is a constant reassessment of the quality of artists, and their relative importance as time passes.

The same diversity of practice was true in the 1950s. The mainstream, as represented by the teaching at the Slade School, where Wonnacott was trained, still believed that the practice of art should involve some level of close observation and depiction of the natural world, as interpreted through the procedures of analytical drawing. The teaching of art was about the discipline of close observation: a training in measured looking, and how the three-dimensional natural world and human figure can, and should, be translated into the two dimensions of drawing and painting. The task and challenge of depiction was expected to be not photographic realism but, instead, a form of acute visual analysis and interpretation of the world and its appearances, a record of looking and perception, some level of pictorial response to one's surroundings, including a strong element of social observation: people mattered; there was still an element of validity in portraiture. This was the realm from which the art of Lucian Freud and Frank Auerbach emerged – the School of London.

What happened to demote, and eventually to more or less eradicate, this idea of the responsibilities of art? In the late 1960s, after Wonnacott had left the Slade and while he was in retreat for a decade after graduating, painting his family in Southend, the central beliefs about art and its responsibilities moved away from any form of representation towards experiment and innovation, with a premium placed on novel ways of thinking about the practice of art, the excitement of new ideas and beliefs, busting all taboos, with inventions and experiments in art being more highly regarded than adherence to, or recognition of, inherited languages and traditions. In particular, there was a shift in 1964 when Bryan Robertson showed his *New Generation* exhibition at the Whitechapel Art Gallery. Most of the artists whose work was shown had been at the Royal College of Art, not the Slade. They regarded the Slade as too high-minded, were much more interested in popular culture than high culture, and were particularly influenced by American art. As Keith Vaughan wrote in his journal at the time:

> After all one's thought and search and effort to make some sort of image which would embody the life of our time, it turns out that all that was really

significant were toffee wrappers, liquorice allsorts and tune-up motor bikes. So one could have saved oneself the trouble. I understand how the stranded dinosaurs must have felt.[79]

It is forgotten that, for much of his career, Lucian Freud, now one of the most celebrated painters of the last 50 years, believed himself to be marginal, unrecognised by the art world, practising a rigorous attitude to painting, day after day, every day being about a new private and personal artistic challenge.

I admire Wonnacott for his consistent determination to adhere to a form of art practice which may no longer be highly regarded or part of the mainstream, but which he believes to be just as important, just as much a responsibility of the artist, as it has been for the last 600 years – the desire to record a version of the world through visual representation, with an element of science in the way he works with perspective as well as of art. He is currently totally out of fashion. Indeed, he never has been in fashion, although once represented by two of the leading Bond Street galleries. But he has painted a version of the world, his world – a scene of water and skies and of the Thames estuary, a great number of commissioned portraits, including *The Royal Family* – which have validity as a way of looking at and documenting the late 20th century: a vision that belongs not so much to the elite of the art world or the avant-garde as to the world beside the Essex shore, far away from the globalised and sometimes over-standardised product of the international art fairs.

Wonnacott depicts the everyday of the Thames estuary and the riverfront, the local park and scenes of his family, not as a photorealist, which he is not, but seen and composed with a powerful feeling of visual interpretation and pictorial invention, shaping his view of his surroundings through a deep interest in the science of perspective, an unusually intense and distinctive form of observational and semi-scientific visual analysis and pictorial record, formidable in the way that it documents its imaginative world.

Art should not always consist only of the front of a torpedo which Alfred H. Barr, Jr (1902–1981), the first Director of the Museum of Modern Art in New York, depicted as moving through history, with those at the front of the torpedo being the only artists worthy of critical attention. The practice of art has always in the past

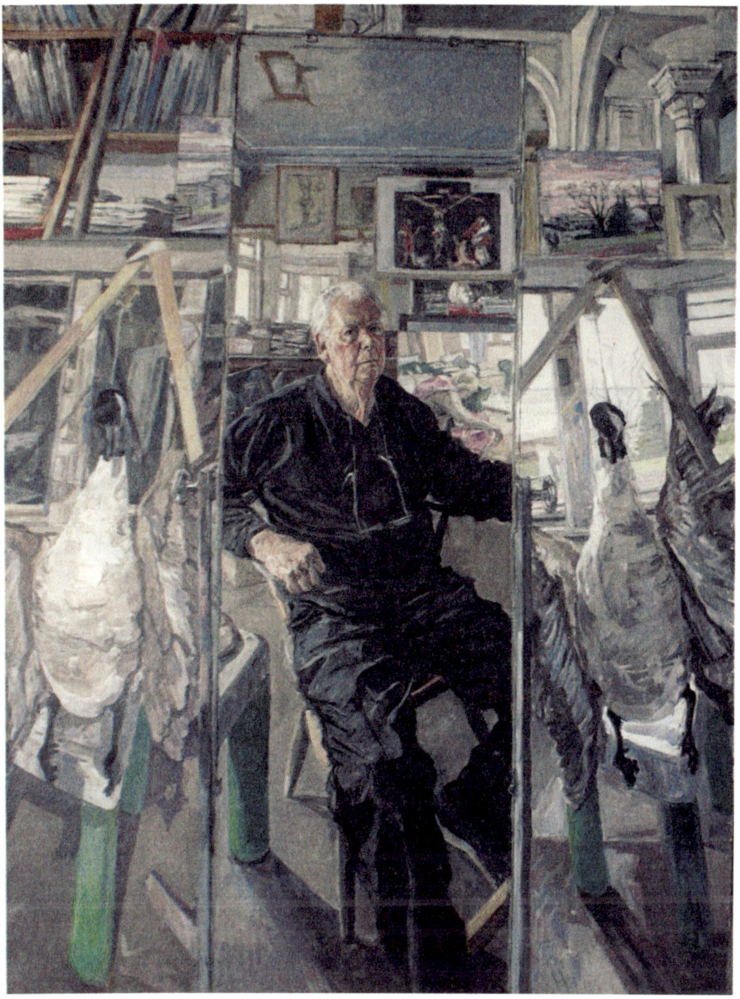

61. *Self-Portrait with Grünewald and Two Geese*, 2018

consisted of different attitudes and approaches to the world, a plurality and diversity of art forms. Realism and naturalism, drawing and composition, representations of the human figure and of nature, landscape, portraiture, food and Essex, should be allowed to play their part in art. Artists have in the past always had a role in structuring and representing the world, subjecting it to a form of analysis and record. If painting is to survive and to continue to develop as a visual discipline for celebrating our consciousness, then artists like Wonnacott, who spend their time in looking at, and thinking about, the nature and status of visual invention, should be highly regarded.

Notes

1 Charles Saumarez Smith, 'A painter of estuary life', in *John Wonnacott: The Estuary*, exh.cat., Focal Point Gallery, Southend-on-Sea, 2019, pp 16–17.

2 Wonnacott, email, 16 June 2020.

3 Wonnacott, email, 19 April 2020.

4 ibid. Johnson's influence is also described in Lynda Morris, 'A conversation with John Wonnacott', in *John Wonnacott: The Estuary*, op.cit., p.6.

5 Wonnacott, email, 19 April 2020.

6 Wonnacott, email, 20 April 2020.

7 ibid.

8 Tristram Hillier, *Leda and the Goose: An Autobiography*, Longman, Green, London, 1954, p.73.

9 Caroline Maclean, *Circles and Squares: The Lives and Art of the Hampstead Modernists*, Bloomsbury, London, 2020, p.206.

10 W.H. Auden, *Letters from Iceland*, Faber and Faber, London, 1937, p.218, and *The Language of Learning and the Language of Love: Uncollected Writing*, Clarendon Press, Oxford, 1994, p.139.

11 I am conscious that this may be an over-simplification of what was a long process of art school reform, but it is based on a perception among artists that it led to the intellectualisation of what was previously a practical discipline. There is more detailed information about the report in Clive Ashwin, *A Century of Art Education 1882–1982*, Middlesex Polytechnic, London, 1982.

12 In general, Wonnacott was happy with my text, apart from these two sentences and their precise wording, which in their current form reflect a number of conversations and email exchanges in June 2020 in order to reflect his views as accurately as possible.

13 Wonnacott, 'From the Slade to Norwich', in *John Wonnacott and John Lessore: The Norwich Life Room*, exh.cat., Norwich Castle Museum, Norwich, 2014, p.17.

14 Wonnacott, email, 21 April 2020.

15 ibid.

16 ibid.

17 Wonnacott, 'From the Slade to Norwich', op.cit., p.27.

18 Catherine Lampert, in *Frank Auerbach: Speaking and Painting*, Thames & Hudson, London, 2015, p.74, says he started in October 1963. Wonnacott remembers him teaching in his third year, which was October 1961. No one can remember which year it was for sure.

19 Catherine Lampert in conversation with Frank Auerbach, email, 21 May 2020.

20 Wonnacott, 'From the Slade to Norwich', op.cit., pp 27–8.

21 Wonnacott, email, 26 April 2020.

22 John Lessore, email, 19 April 2020.

23 I am conscious that the use of the term 'School of London' is contested and that art historians, as well as the artists themselves, have resisted it; but it remains a useful portmanteau term for the group of figurative artists who were labelled and exhibited as such during the 1980s and 1990s, including in the Royal Academy's exhibition *British Art of the Twentieth Century* (1987), the British Council's *A School of London: Six Figurative Artists* (1987) and Alistair Hicks, *School of London: The Resurgence of Contemporary Painting*, Phaidon, London, 1989. There is an account of the use of the term in James Hyman, *The Battle for Realism: Figurative Art in Britain during the Cold War, 1945–1960*, Yale University Press, London, 2001, pp 6–7.

24 Bruce Bernard, 'Painter friends', in *From London*, exh.cat., British Council, London, 1995, p.50.

25 The best recent studies of the nature of Essex and its peculiarities appear in Rachel Lichtenstein, *Estuary: Out from London to the Sea*, Hamish Hamilton, London, 2016, and Gillian Darley, *Excellent Essex: In Praise of England's Most Misunderstood County*, Old Street Publishing, London, 2019.

26 Wonnacott, email, 19 April 2020.

27 Morris, 'A conversation with John Wonnacott', op.cit., p.5.

28 Wonnacott, email, 19 April 2020.

29 Wonnacott, 'From the Slade to Norwich', op.cit., p.28.

30 Morris, 'A conversation with John Wonnacott', op.cit., p.7.

31 Andrew Forge, letter of invitation, 28 August 1973 (Hayward Gallery archive 1973-08-28).

32 Wonnacott, email, 4 June 2020.

33 Giles Auty, 'Director line to the past', *Spectator*, 23 March 1985. I am grateful to Gill Turner of the London Library for her help in locating this quotation.

34 For the 1975 Summer Exhibition and its selection committee, see William Packer, 'Into the Fray', *The Royal Academy Summer Exhibition: A Chronicle, 1769–2018* (www.chronicle250.com).

35 Morris, 'A conversation with John Wonnacott', op.cit., p.4.

36 *The Human Clay: An Exhibition Selected by R.B. Kitaj*, exh.cat., Hayward Gallery, London, 1976.

37 William Feaver, 'The room with a view', *Observer*, 21 December 1980.

38 Marina Vaizey, 'Life in our time', *Sunday Times*, 21 December 1980.

39 John Wonnacott in conversation with Richard Cork, quoted in Martin Gayford, 'Introduction', in *Recent Paintings: John Wonnacott*, exh.cat., Agnew's, London, 1996.

40 Richard Cork, 'Pressure of feeling', in *The School of London and Their Friends: The Collection of Elaine and Melvin Merians*, exh.cat., Yale Center for British Art, New Haven, CT, 2000, p.15.

41 *The School of London and Their Friends*, op.cit., pp 112–13.

42 Feaver, 'The room with a view', op.cit.

43 Vaizey, 'Life in our time', op.cit.

44 The phrase 'mysterious conventionality' was first used to describe Michael Andrews's work in an article by David Sylvester, 'Michael Andrews: Mysterious conventionality', *Sunday Times*, 13 January 1963, p.15.

45 Lynda Morris, 'Introduction', in *John Wonnacott and John Lessore*, op.cit., p.10.

46 ibid.

47 Vaizey, 'Life in our time', op.cit.

48 Morris, 'Introduction', op.cit., p.13.

49 Tate Gallery, catalogue entry, *The Norwich School of Art*, https://www.tate.org.uk/art/artworks/wonnacott-the-norwich-school-of-art-t03928.

50 ibid.

51 Richard Shone, 'The Hard-Won Image', *Burlington Magazine*, October 1984, p.651.

52 Richard Morphet, 'Le Réalisme anglais entre les deux guerres', *Cahiers du Musée National d'Art Moderne*, nos 7–8, 1981.

53 John Lessore, email, 19 April 2020.

54 The phrase 'like an Expulsion from Paradise' comes from a series of conversations with the artist recorded in Tate's online catalogue entry for the painting (https://www.tate.org.uk/art/artworks/wonnacott-the-norwich-school-of-art-t03928).

55 John Russell Taylor, 'Conflicting pulls of recognition', *The Times*, 12 March 1985.

56 Wonnacott, artist's statement, August 1988.

57 Wonnacott, email, 1 May 2020.

58 ibid.

59 Robin Gibson, *Painting the Century: 101 Portrait Masterpieces 1900–2000*, exh.cat., National Portrait Gallery, London, 2000, p.236.

60 Wonnacott, email, 13 May 2020.

61 William Feaver, 'Introduction', in *John Wonnacott's East Anglian Coast*, exh.cat., Christchurch Mansion, Ipswich, 1998, p.5.

62 This description of the purpose of the commission appears in the Royal Museums Greenwich online catalogue entry for the painting (https://www.rmg.co.uk/collections/objects/rmgc-object-201231).

63 Wonnacott, email, 13 May 2020.

64 Royal Museums Greenwich, Online Collections Website (www.rsmg.org.uk).

65 Simon Schama, *Landscape and Memory*, Alfred A. Knopf, New York, 1995, p.3, quoted in Ken Worpole, *350 Miles: An Essex Journey*, Essex Regeneration Agency, Colchester, 2005, n.p.

66 Jason Orton and Ken Worpole, *The New English Landscape*, Field Station, London, 2013, p.13.

67 Wonnacott, email, 15 May 2020.

68 Charles Saumarez Smith, 'Royal Portraits at the National Portrait Gallery', in *The Royal Family: A Centenary Portrait*, exh.cat., National Portrait Gallery, London, 2000, p.15.

69 Charles Saumarez Smith to Sir Robert Fellowes, 31 July 1998 (NPG Archive).

70 Martin Gayford, interview for the *Daily Telegraph*. I am grateful to Martin Gayford for giving me access to his interview transcript.

71 ibid.

72 Wonnacott, email, 15 May 2020.

73 For Manton's life, see Nicholas Serota, 'Edwin Manton', *Guardian*, 17 October 2005.

74 Wonnacott, email, 15 May 2020.

75 These comments come from the artist's notes on his website (www.johnwonnacott.co.uk).

76 John Wonnacott, email, 26 May 2020.

77 Ernst Gombrich, *The Story of Art*, 12th edn, Phaidon Press, London, 1984, p.483.

78 Patrick Elliott and Sasha Llewellyn, *True to Life: British Realist Painting in the 1920s and 1930s*, exh.cat., National Galleries of Scotland, Edinburgh, 2017, esp. pp 9–20.

79 Keith Vaughan, *Journal and Drawings 1939–1965*, A. Ross, London, 1966, p.198, quoted in Lisa Tickner, *London's New Scene: Art and Culture in the 1960s*, Yale University Press, New Haven and London, 2020, p.335.

Select Exhibitions

British Painting '74, London, Hayward Gallery, 1974

John Wonnacott, Colchester, The Minories, 1977

John Wonnacott: Paintings and Drawings, Rochdale, Rochdale Art Gallery, 1978

John Wonnacott First London Exhibition, London, Marlborough Fine Art, 1980

The Hard-Won Image: Traditional Method and Subject in Recent British Art, London, Tate Gallery, 1984

John Wonnacott: Recent Work, London, Marlborough Fine Art, 1985

John Wonnacott: Recent Work, London, Marlborough Fine Art, 1988

The Pursuit of the Real: British Figurative Painting from Sickert to Bacon, Manchester, Manchester City Art Galleries, 1990

John Wonnacott: Recent Paintings, London, Agnew's, 1992

Contemporary Portraits from Suffolk to Essex, Sudbury, Gainsborough's House, 1995

Recent Paintings: John Wonnacott, London, Agnew's, 1996

John Wonnacott's East Anglian Coast, Ipswich, Christchurch Mansion, 1998

John Wonnacott: An Exhibition in New York and London, New York, Hirschl and Adler, 1999, and London, Agnew's, 2000

Painting the Century: 101 Portrait Masterpieces 1900–2000, London, National Portrait Gallery, 2000

The Royal Family: A Centenary Portrait, London, National Portrait Gallery, 2000

John Wonnacott: Bankside and Other Buildings, London, Art Space Gallery, 2000

The School of London and Their Friends: The Collection of Elaine and Melvin Merians, New Haven, CT, Yale Center for British Art, 2000

John Wonnacott: Recent Paintings, London, Agnew's, 2005

John Wonnacott: A Tale of Two Houses, London, Agnew's, 2011

John Wonnacott and John Lessore: The Norwich Life Room, Norwich, Norwich Castle Museum, 2014

John Wonnacott: The Estuary, Southend-on-Sea, Focal Point Gallery, 2019

Select Bibliography

Auty, Giles, 'John Wonnacott: A 50-year retrospective of self-portraits', *British Art Journal*, 13:3, 2012, p.127.

Feaver, William, 'Introduction', in *John Wonnacott's East Anglian Coast*, exh.cat., Christchurch Mansion, Ipswich, 1998.

Gayford, Martin, 'Portrait of John Major', *Spectator*, 20 September 1997, pp 46–7.

———, 'John Wonnacott's East Anglia', *Spectator*, 25 April 1998, p.48.

Gibson, Robin, *The Portrait Now*, exh.cat., National Portrait Gallery, London, 1993.

Gombrich, E.H., 'Mirror and map: Theories of artistic representation', *Philosophical Transactions of the Royal Society of London*, 270:903, 1975, pp 119–49.

Hicks, Alistair, *School of London: The Resurgence of Contemporary Painting*, Phaidon, London, 1989.

Hyman, James, *The Battle for Realism: Figurative Art in Britain during the Cold War, 1945–1960*, Yale University Press, London, 2001.

Morris, Lynda, 'A conversation with John Wonnacott', in *John Wonnacott: The Estuary*, exh.cat., Focal Point Gallery, Southend-on-Sea, 2019.

Neve, Christopher, *Unquiet Landscape: Places and Ideas in Twentieth-Century British Landscape Painting*, Faber and Faber, London, 1990.

Saumarez Smith, Charles, 'A painter of estuary life', in *John Wonnacott: The Estuary*, exh.cat., Focal Point Gallery, Southend-on-Sea, 2019, pp 16–17.

Tickner, Lisa, *London's New Scene: Art and Culture in the 1960s*, Yale University Press, London and New Haven, CT, 2020.

Acknowledgements

I wrote this book with John Wonnacott's encouragement and, as will have been obvious throughout the text and particularly the endnotes, a great deal of help from him in answering questions, sending long emails providing detailed information about the circumstances of individual works, fleshing out the narrative, and correcting the final text with meticulous attention to every detail. I regard him as in many ways co-author. I have also been much encouraged by the support and critical encouragement of Jonathan Mantle, Dick Humphreys and Antje Southern for the project and for their helpful reading of the text. A number of Wonnacott's friends, allies and supporters have also provided information or read the text, including William Feaver, Martin Gayford, Catherine Lampert, John Lessore and John Tancock, and I greatly benefited from a tough reading of the text by Cathy Courtney, who took a red pencil to its redundancies. Once I had completed the book, it became obvious that it could only be published with a subsidy and I am enormously grateful that it was made possible by a most generous gift. Lucy Clark, the commissioning editor of Lund Humphries, has been consistently helpful and patient in making all the necessary arrangements for publication and Rochelle Roberts has been incredibly helpful in sorting out the reproducibility and reproduction rights of all the illustrations. Anna Norman oversaw the production, Robert Davies did the copy-editing and Jason Wolfe and Luke Hall the design. I thank them all.

Picture Credits

p.6 *Self-Portrait, Summer Morning, The Red Shirt*, 2003–5, oil on board, 61 × 50.8 cm (24 × 20 in), artist's collection

1 *Temptation*, 1953–4, poster paint on sugar paper, 58.4 × 83.8 cm (23 × 33 in), artist's collection

2 *Self-Portrait*, 1956, pencil on paper, 27.9 × 20.3 cm (11 × 8 in), artist's collection

3 *Gwen with Reginald*, 1957, pencil on paper, 27.9 × 20.3 cm (11 × 8 in), artist's collection

4 *The White Nude, Marjorie*, 1959, oil on board, 76 × 61 cm (30 × 24 in), private collection

5 *Cooking Apples*, 1962, oil on board, 40.6 × 45.7 cm (16 × 18 in), artist's collection

6 Michael Andrews, *The Family in the Garden*, 1960–62, oil on canvas, 200 × 300 cm (78 ¾ × 118 in), Centro de Arte Moderna José de Azeredo Perdigao, Fundaçao Calouste Gulbenkian, Lisbon, inv. PE270

7 *The Family*, 1963–74, oil on board, 183 × 518.1 cm (72 × 204 in), artist's collection

8 *Crescent Road 1*, 1964–6, oil on board, 121.9 × 183 cm (48 × 72 in), artist's collection

9 *Crescent Road*, 1963–76, oil on plywood, 176 × 183 cm (69 ¼ × 72 in), Rochdale Art Gallery

10 Three studies for *The Family, Whole Painting 2*, 1970, drawing, total size 30.5 × 76.2 cm (12 × 30 in), artist's collection

11 *Watching the Grandfather*, sketch for *The Family*, *c.*1970, oil on board, 121.9 × 167.6 cm (48 × 66 in), artist's collection

12 *Winter on Marine Parade*, 1972–4, oil on board, 91.4 × 121.9 cm (36 × 48 in), private collection

13 *Elms and Trellis, Marine Parade*, 1962, oil on board, 93 × 112 cm (36 ½ × 44 in), Government Art Collection. Purchased from the London Group exhibition, April 1963, inv. 6059

14 *Small Self-Portrait*, 1963–5, oil on board, 30.5 × 30.5 cm (12 × 12 in), artist's collection

15 *Self-Portrait with Electric Light Bulb*, 1964–71, oil on board, 183 × 76 cm (72 × 30 in), Collection Jan Krugier

16 *The Grandfather*, 1967–9, oil on board, 243.8 × 121.9 cm (96 × 48 in), Collection Elaine Merians

17 *Trees on Marine Parade with Anne Sleeping*, 1972–4, oil on board, 91.4 × 121.9 cm (36 × 48 in), artist's collection

18 *Three Estuary Windows*, 1977–80, oil on canvas, 96.5 × 259 cm (39 × 102 in) each, artist's collection

19 *Estuary, the Goat*, 1976–8, oil on board, 76.2 × 121.9 cm (30 × 48 in), anonymous collection

20 *Estuary, the Steps*, 1976–7, oil on board, 121.9 × 91.4 cm (48 × 36 in), anonymous collection

21 *The Life Room*, 1977–80, oil on canvas, 173 × 259 cm (68 × 102 in), Norwich Castle Museum and Art Gallery

22 *Lynda*, 1982–4, oil on board, 34 × 28.3 cm (13 ⅜ × 11 ⅛ in), private collection

23 *Norwich Cathedral*, 1981–5, oil on canvas, 167.6 × 275 cm (66 × 108 ¼ in), artist's collection

24 *Norwich School of Art*, 1982–4, oil on canvas, 193.5 × 264.8 (76 ¼ × 104 ¼ in), Tate Gallery, London

25 *The Foreshore Superintendent's Hut*, 1981–4, oil on canvas, 117.5 × 153.7 cm (46 ¼ × 60 ½ in), private collection

26 *The Palace Hotel, Southend*, 1983–97, oil on canvas, 244.8 × 244.8 cm (96 ⅜ × 96 ⅜ in), artist's collection

27 *The Ladies' Bowling Green*, 1981–5, oil on canvas, 82.6 × 122 cm (32 ½ × 48 in), Collection of Brian and Brenda Curtoise

28 *The Hard*, 1985–8, oil on canvas, 73.6 × 197.5 cm (29 × 77 ¾ in), private collection

29 *Red Lifebelt, Chalkwell Beach, from the Promenade Looking to Kent*, 1990, oil on board, 96.5 × 208.3 cm (38 × 82 in), artist's collection

30 *Mud Pool with Collie*, 1985–8, oil on canvas, 61 × 121.9 cm (24 × 48 in), private collection

31 *Chalkwell Beach, Floodwater Overflow, Late Afternoon*, 1989–92, oil on board, 61 × 122 cm (24 × 48 in), British Council

32 *Night Portrait with Blue Easel*, 1990–1, oil on masonite, 215.3 × 114.9 cm (84 ¾ × 45 ¼ in), Metropolitan Museum of Art, New York, Purchase, Lila Acheson Wallace Gift, 1993

33 *Studio Conversation I*, 1993–4, oil on fibreboard, 244.1 × 122.2 cm (96 × 48 in), Tate Gallery, London

34 *Sir Adam Thomson*, 1985–6, oil on board, 243.9 × 243.9 cm (96 × 96 in), Scottish National Portrait Gallery, inv. 2697

35 *Study for John Major*, 1997, pencil, 84.2 × 59.4 cm (33 ⅛ × 23 ⅜ in), National Portrait Gallery, London, NPG 6410(6)

36 *The Rt. Hon. Sir John Major, Downing Street*, 1997, oil on board, 218 × 152.7 cm (85 ¾ × 60 in), National Portrait Gallery, London, NPG 6402

37 *Shingle Laboratory No.1*, 1994–6, oil on board, 91.4 × 121.9 cm (36 × 48 in), artist's collection

38 *Shingle Laboratory No.2 with Orford Church and Castle*, 1994–6, oil on board, 91.4 × 121.9 cm (36 × 48 in), National Trust

39 *Laboratory Pagodas Nos 4 & 5, Late Summer, Orford Ness*, 1992–5, oil on board, 94 × 122.2 cm (37 × 48 ⅛ in), artist's collection

40 *Estuary Mudflats: The Battle*, 1994–8, oil on canvas, 152.4 × 152.4 cm (60 × 60 in), artist's collection

41 *Winter Afternoon, Container Ships off Felixstowe*, 1993–4, oil on panel, 151.9 × 200 cm (60 × 78 ¾ in), National Maritime Museum, Greenwich, London, BHC 4249

42 *Estuary Crowstone: The Overflow with Girl about to Cartwheel*, 1998, oil on board, 335.2 × 199 cm (132 × 78 ¼ in), private collection

43 *Estuary, the Paddling Pool with Zofja Throwing Stones*, 1995–6, oil on board, 68.6 × 126.3 cm (27 × 50 in), private collection

44 *Admiral of the Fleet, Lord Lewin of Greenwich, in the Painted Hall*, 1995–8, oil on board, 199 × 335.2 cm (78 ¼ × 132 in), National Maritime Museum, Greenwich, London, ZBA 0731

45 *Head of Prince William II*, 1999–2000, oil on board, 41.9 × 29.2 cm (16 ½ × 11 ½ in), private collection

46 *Study for Prince Harry*, 1999–2000, pencil on paper, 58.4 × 40.6 cm (23 × 16 in), private collection

47 *The Royal Family: A Centenary Portrait*, 2000, oil on canvas, 366.3 × 249.3 cm (144 ¼ × 98 ⅛ in), National Portrait Gallery, London, NPG 6479

48 *Night Portrait, Black Jersey*, 1989–92, oil on board, 76.5 × 61.3 cm (30 ⅛ × 24 ⅛ in), artist's collection

49 *Small Portrait, Met Study*, 1992–5, oil on board, 63.5 × 45.7 cm (25 × 18 in), private collection

50 *Self-Portrait, Winter Sunset*, 2004–5, oil on board, 45.7 × 38.1 cm (18 × 15 in), artist's collection

51 *The Mathematician I*, 1990–91, oil on board, 121.9 × 64.8 cm (48 × 25 ½ in), private collection

52 *Red Tablecloth II, Oyster Eaters*, 1996–9, oil on board, 121.9 × 152.4 cm (48 × 60 in), private collection

53 *Portrait of Jim Manton*, 2000, oil on canvas, 610 × 510 cm (240 ¼ × 201 in), Tate Gallery, London

54 *Ian with Striped Shirt*, 1991–2, oil on board, 50.2 × 34.9 cm (19 ¾ × 13 ¾ in), artist's collection

55 *The Mathematician, Professor Bernard de Neumann*, 2001–4, oil on board, 152.4 × 121.9 cm (60 × 48 in), artist's collection

56 *Putting on Ballet Shoe 2, Young Dancers Prepare for Class while Seniors Practise Jumps*, 2008–10, oil on canvas, 100.3 × 95.9 cm (39 ½ × 37 ¾ in), artist's collection

57 *Taipans on the 48th Floor*, 2012–13, oil on canvas, 121.9 × 152.4 cm (48 × 60 in), Collection Jardine Matheson

58 *Self-Portrait with an Apple for G*, 2017, oil on canvas, 36.8 × 36.8 cm (14 ½ × 14 ½ in), artist's collection

59 *Hanging Goose, Day*, 2017, oil on board, 152.4 × 121.9 cm (60 × 48 in), artist's collection

60 *Grenfell Tower, Winter*, 2017–18, oil on canvas, 213.4 × 159.5 cm (84 × 62 ¾ in), artist's collection

61 *Self-Portrait with Grünewald and Two Geese*, 2018, oil on board, 121.9 × 91.4 cm (48 × 36 in), artist's collection

Index

List of Works